The NATURALLY HEALTHY TRAVELER

*Effective Solutions for Common
Ailments on the Road and at Home*

Susan W. Kramer, Ph.D., RH (AHG), CCH

LOTUS PRESS

P.O. Box 325
Twin Lakes, WI 53181 USA

1st edition - October 2001 (Aspen Press)
2nd revised edition, 2012

Published by

LOTUS
PRESS

Lotus Press
P.O. Box 325
Twin Lakes, WI 53181 USA
800-824-6396 (toll free order phone)
262-889-8561 (office phone)
262-889-2461 (office fax)
www.lotuspress.com (website)
lotuspress@lotuspress.com (email)

Edited by Phyllis Mueller

The trademarks contained within are the property of their respective
owners.

Printed in the United States of America.
ISBN: 978-0-9409-8504-9
Formerly published under ISBN: 0-9713431-5-2 (Aspen Press)

10 9 8 7 6 5 4 3 2 1

PRAISE FOR
The Naturally Healthy Traveler

"*The Naturally Healthy Traveler* is fantastic — fun, practical, and medically accurate. From now on, I'm not leaving home without it. It's going to have a permanent home in my carry-on luggage."
Christiane Northrup, M.D.
Author of *The Wisdom of Menopause* and *Women's Bodies, Women's Wisdom*

"An entertaining little book packed with big ideas, full of proven remedies to prevent and relieve the stress and strain of travel. Tremendous. Take it along. You may wish you had if you don't!"
James Duke, Ph.D.
Author of *The Green Pharmacy*

"A treasure trove of good ideas and common sense for travelers who want to stay healthy while minimizing their use of pharmaceuticals."
Theresa Graedon, Ph.D.
Co-author of *The People's Pharmacy Guide to Home and Herbal Remedies*

"*The Naturally Healthy Traveler* is not only very informative and extremely useful, but also great fun to read. It provides quick remedies along with important preparation guidance to prevent the most common ills encountered when traveling. Highly recommended!"
Lesley Tierra, L.Ac., AHG
Author of *Healing With the Herbs of Life*
Co-founder, American Herbalists Guild

"This book should be available in every airport terminal, train or bus station, and seaport. Pack it in your bag. It offers valuable preventive measures and conventional, herbal, homeopathic, and other natural approaches."

Michael Tierra, OMD
Author of *The Way of Herbs*
Founder, American Herbalists Guild

"I enjoy The Naturally Healthy Traveler as much for its awesome adventure tales, as I do for its eminently practical and useful advice."

Rosemary Gladstar
Author of *Medicinal Herbs: A Beginner's Guide*

"Most of us love to travel, experiencing exotic locals, new cultures, interesting sights and delightful and unusual foods. The benefits of travel, whether domestic or foreign, are significant but so are the downsides. [Think of] altitude sickness at Machu Picchu, Delhi belly in India, jet lag in Istanbul or a nasty cold in San Francisco. You are far from home and your doctor, what do you do? Packing Susan Kramer's wonderful book, The Natural Healthy Traveler in your suitcase could make the difference between a wonderful vacation and one you would rather forget. Don't leave home without it!"

David Winston, RH(AHG)
Author of *Adaptogens: Herbs for Strength, Stamina, and Stress Relief and Herbal Therapy and Supplements*

"Good solid information ... an excellent companion for every traveler's suitcase!"

Miranda Castro, RSHom
Author of *The Complete Homeopathy Handbook and The Homeopathic Guide to Stress*

Dedication
To all my teachers

Acknowledgements

To my mother, Madeline Kramer, I am grateful for your gentle humor, your knowledge, and your acceptance of all my endeavors. To my late father, Eugene Kramer, "The Chief," an avid traveler who was always of service and who believed I could do anything, thank you.

Thanks to those who looked me straight in the eye and told me to start writing. To my teachers, Lesley and Michael Tierra of the East West School of Herbology, who advised me to begin book writing on the very first day we met and have continued encouraging me to this day, thank you.

Thank you to Mark Blumenthal, the founder and Executive Director of the American Botanical Council and a true mensch, for invaluable assistance in the publication of this book.

For innumerable contributions, I am most grateful to Juaquita Callaway, Miranda Castro, Frenesa Hall, Patricia Kilpatrick, Lisa Larsen-Moss, Ronda Reynolds, Libby Eason, Kas Sheehan, and Dana Ullman.

To my friend and editor, Phyllis Mueller, who shared my vision, produced the first edition of this book, graciously accepted my lacunae, and provided unwavering support and technical expertise, my heartfelt thanks. To Bonnie Supplee, who created the wonderful design that perfectly matched my vision of this book, thank you. Thanks to Sonja Benjamin, Solange Bonnet, Tania

Machado, and Mara Orlando — my language teachers — for the assistance with the Foreign Phrases.

Finally, I acknowledge all of you who read this book and use it to improve the quality of your life and travels. Thank you.

Susan W. Kramer
November 1, 2012
Atlanta, Georgia

Table of Contents

Introduction

I always wanted a travel guide that would tell me what to do when emergencies, illnesses, and accidents arose. Like coughing up blood when preparing to dive the Great Barrier Reef. Dealing with the inevitable constipation at conferences. Driving cross-country with a companion who became car sick on winding roads. At a remote country inn, my Dad running out of his needed water pill. A friend with food poisoning who was vomiting. Me with food poisoning and diarrhea. Arriving in Colorado Springs for the Olympic Trials and feeling the altitude. Climbing Mt. Kilimanjaro and experiencing altitude sickness. Dogbite while trekking in Tibet. Difficulty falling asleep or staying asleep. Tossing and turning all night. Feeling tired. I looked for over 30 years, but I never found the guide I wanted. So I decided to write one, to provide the information a traveler is likely to need in one convenient, accessible place.

I chose an easy-to-read format to help you find the information you are looking for without more stress. It is written in layperson's language with a minimum of medical jargon. It explains, step by step, how to deal with different problems. This handbook has the answers you need, emphasizing inexpensive, easy-to-find, and easy-to-pack natural solutions and where to obtain them. It includes information on common travel ailments that can ruin a trip—ailments such as constipation, jet lag, stiffness, and blisters. I made it entertaining because I never liked those dry-as-dust medical books.

We have health problems when we travel that we rarely or never have at home. Because we don't have these problems at home, we don't think of them when we prepare to travel. This guide reminds you of common travel ailments so that you can plan ahead and assists you with travel solutions to problems you may not have anticipated.

Travel ailments can differ from at-home health problems because diet, clothing, schedule, and environment change with travel. We lose many of our anchors, many of our constants. Air travel exposes us to desert-dry air, decreased oxygen, and lower atmospheric pressure. Changing time zones upsets our internal clocks. We tend to do too much. We lift too much, talk too much, eat and drink too much. Increased quantities of food, salt, sugar, and fat, the hallmarks of most restaurant meals, all affect our digestion.

Travel involves change, and change is stressful. Increased levels of stress during travel increase the likelihood of illness. Stress exacerbates everything; many problems appear only under stress. People who never get sick fall ill. Athletes experience unexpected fatigue. Sound sleepers cannot fall asleep, and sometimes they cannot stay asleep. Normally relaxed people become tense and anxious. Eating while under increased stress plays havoc with digestion. Travel is stressful even under the best of circumstances, and not feeling your best makes it more stressful. The increased stress of travel creates many of the problems that you commonly experience during travel, but rarely experience otherwise.

The Naturally Healthy Traveler addresses travel ailments and their solutions. Major topics are organized into chapters. Each chapter includes personal experiences; specific instructions; food, herbal, homeopathic, and drug store remedies; and handy chapter summaries. When you need assistance with a travel problem, look first to the chapter headings. Alternatively, look up words relating to your problem in the index at the back of the book.

The remedies I selected for this book work well. They are drawn from eastern and western herbalism, homeopathy, and western allopathic medicine. The information in this book has been assembled from a variety of sources — personal experience, research of the medical and healthcare literature, advice and counsel of health professionals, and numerous case studies. Sometimes travelers know precisely what they need but that product (or healthcare tradition) may not be available for hundreds of miles — *The Naturally Healthy Traveler* assists you in finding effective substitutes. I firmly believe that "the herb you need grows in your own backyard." To paraphrase, you can find a remedy close at hand, wherever you are in the world.

No matter how much I have learned over the years, when I am suffering, I find that all my education and knowledge disappears. My idea is that this travel guide will stay packed in your luggage, and that you'll find it so useful that you will remove it only to read when preparing for travel or for entertainment or information while traveling. It's meant to be handy. And it's affordable, so you can buy copies to give to friends who are planning trips. It is my hope that *The Naturally Healthy Traveler* addresses all your problems and answers all of your questions.

Happy, healthy traveling!

Susan

ALTITUDE SICKNESS

I had the great good fortune of climbing Mt. Kilimanjaro to celebrate my 50th birthday. Climbing Mt. Kilimanjaro takes days of hiking at high to extremely high altitude with temperatures that range from minus 20 degrees F. to over 100 degrees F. Challenging? Yes, but it was worth it to share this adventure with a lifelong friend, to see the legendary snows of Kilimanjaro, and to experience the exhilaration of the climb.

In preparation, we trained for 12 months—walking 5 miles daily, walking 12 to 15 miles each week with a pack, and hiking local hills and mountains. We lifted weights and cycled. We knew we could not train for altitude, but we knew that getting in the best possible physical condition would improve our prospects of completing the climb.

We arrived in Tanzania and spent a day meeting with our guide to review the climb itinerary, to discuss safety and climbing, and to confirm that we had all the necessary gear. The next morning we took a 4-hour jeep ride on dusty dirt roads to the mountain. Our 11-person climbing crew was waiting for us when we arrived at Rongai Gate. We looked around but could not see a mountain—we saw only farm fields. We asked our guide to point out Kilimanjaro; he laughed and said, "Here. We are on it. You cannot see it; let us go now!"

We walked uphill through fields that abruptly ended in a rain forest. We plunged rapidly into the trees as we followed a wide, park-like path. We were hiking in deep shade; the temperature was in the high 80s, and we were working hard. I tried to control my breathing and felt myself getting hot. The trees ended, and we emerged into bush country. The air was thinning, and we had

11

not yet finished our first day! We arrived at Simba Camp, at 8,700 feet, removed our packs, and set up camp. We were ready to rest, but our guide instructed us to set off on our own, to hike an additional hour up the trail and then return. "Hike high, sleep low"— this was to assist us with acclimatization. We coughed a little, and we both had mild headaches, but we were very excited.

At the beginning of the second day we could see the mountain for the first time, crowned with snow! I was surprised at my lack of appetite after the past day's exertion. We ate breakfast quickly and resumed our rapid climb.

I don't remember much about the second, third, or fourth days of our climb. We walked rapidly, and I found myself panting from the exertion. Despite the spectacular scenery, my enthusiasm was dissipating. I felt nauseated. My head hurt. My guts hurt. My lungs burned, and I began to cough. Ahead of me, my friend chatted happily with our guide as they strode ahead. I lagged behind. The nausea turned to vomiting. No one knew, and I wasn't going to tell. Surely this would pass.

We ascended to 14,200 feet, our camp for the next 18 hours. We were literally in the clouds, and I could see only a few feet in front of me. Here, at Mawenzi Tarn, we would rest and further acclimatize.

I walked alone. Suddenly, a woman emerged from the mist. She looked beautiful and happy, not at all how I felt! She, the leader of another group, had arrived at our camp 3 hours after my group. She expressed how happy she was and asked how I was doing. "Miserable," I told her. Under her concerned questioning, I told of vomiting trail-side, having no appetite, and feeling air-hunger, burning lungs and eyes, foggy brain, and malaise. I confessed that I feared I had not trained enough and that was why I was sick. I desperately wanted to

12

continue — I did not want to be sent down the mountain. She asked how I had trained and then for our departure and arrival times from and at camp for each day of the climb. She laughed upon hearing our Kilimanjaro climbing schedule.

"*Poli - poli*" she said, and laughed. "*Poli - poli.* Haven't you heard this?"

No, I had not, and I was not in the mood for laughter.

She gripped my shoulders, "My dear," she told me, "you did not under-train, you were walking too fast." She explained *poli - poli* is Swahili for "slowly, slowly." She said that if people fail to travel slowly at altitude, they suffer from altitude sickness. She also said that if I rested long enough and then hiked at the proper speed I would be fine. She then taught me how to walk at altitude—slowly—so I would acclimatize as I walked.

The next morning she was gone. I still felt queasy, but my confidence was high. My friend and our guide left rapidly on a morning hike. Later, I set off on my own. This time though, *poli - poli* . I began climbing into the surrounding hills. At the slower pace, I did not tire. My queasiness passed. I felt OK! This was amazing! I climbed to the top of the nearby ridge, sat down, admired the view, took photos, and ate a snack. Back to normal.

The next day, we broke camp and resumed climbing. This time, I was first! We all hiked *poli - poli* at my new and slower pace. Sure, it was tough. We struggled, we tired, we got hungry and sore. We got snowed on, trudged through sleet, and experienced whiteout conditions. But we did NOT get altitude sickness. In the end, we both made it to the top! *Poli - poli* works!

What Happens at High Altitude?

When altitude increases, air pressure decreases,

resulting in less oxygen available for breathing. For example, at 8,000 feet the amount of oxygen drops to half the amount available at sea level. The decrease in oxygen in the air you're breathing means less oxygen reaches the blood. In response, people naturally begin to breathe more rapidly. Rapid breathing — in typically dry air — results in a loss of moisture.

When air pressure decreases, any pockets of air within the body increase in size, and may cause pain. Surgery often results in temporary pockets of air in the body that may persist for a week or more. If you recently have had surgery, even minor surgery, you may wish to delay activities involving rapid changes in air pressure, such as flying, climbing, or diving.

The increase in altitude also causes fluid in the blood to move into the body tissues, resulting in "thicker" blood and puffy wrists and ankles. You will retain water and may experience swelling in other areas of your body. Fluid also enters the lungs, resulting in coughing and pneumonia-like symptoms.

At higher altitude your risk of sunburn increases. At first, you may not notice the heat of the sun because the temperature tends to drop with increases in altitude. This can be even worse if you are climbing in snow or glacier areas where you will receive both direct and reflected sun rays. Even if clouds obstruct the sun, daytime rays come through. When planning for high altitude, plan for protection against the blazing sun, and cover up.

What Is Altitude Sickness?

Altitude sickness is the constellation of symptoms that result from experiencing high altitude or a rapid increase in altitude. These symptoms are related to the decrease of oxygen in the blood, the loss of moisture, and the slowing of waste elimination. Although not everyone will experience them all, symptoms include headache, nausea and vomiting, loss of appetite, insomnia, breathlessness, bleeding, coughing, anxiety or panic, inability to focus, disorientation, dizziness, and rapid heart rate.

The first signs of altitude sickness are decreased exercise performance and taking more breaths while at rest.

What Is High Altitude?

High altitude ranges from 4,950 to 11,500 feet (1,500–3,500 meters) above sea level.

Very high altitude ranges from 11,500 to 18,050 feet (3,500–5,500 meters) above sea level.

Extreme altitude includes all altitude above 18,050 feet (5,500 meters) above sea level.

How Bad Can Altitude Sickness Get?

You can die from altitude sickness. No joke.

Who Gets Altitude Sickness?

Anyone can get altitude sickness when he or she ascends or stays at sufficiently high altitude. Mountain climbers. Trekkers. Automobile passengers. Visitors to ski resorts. Airline passengers (most jets are pressurized to the equivalent of an 8,000 foot altitude).

Travel communities that commonly deal with altitude sickness include trekkers in Peru, mountain climbers and trekkers in Nepal and the Himalayas, and visitors to Kathmandu.

Preventing Altitude Sickness

The best way to deal with altitude sickness is to avoid it. The medical mountaineering community has amassed considerable knowledge in this area. It is generally agreed that you cannot train for high altitude except by experiencing high altitude. (General physical conditioning may help you to better process oxygen.)

You also cannot "save up" high altitude conditioning for more than a few days—once you descend from a height you begin losing your conditioning. Many experts recommend that you rest at an altitude at which you do not experience altitude sickness for at least 24–48 hours before ascending further.

When ascending above 8,000 feet, preferably limit your ascent to 1,000–2,000 feet per day, with a 24 hour rest every 2–3 days. Yes, this is conservative. Mountaineers commonly recommend that you ascend 2,000–3,000 feet per day. If you are experiencing even mild symptoms, immediately descend. Descending even 500–1,000 feet may be sufficient to stop the symptoms.

Let's say you are visiting Colorado Springs, which sits at approximately 8,000 feet. You've been there two days and you plan to climb Pike's Peak, which is approximately 14,000 feet. If you take the spectacular drive to the top, you can ascend 6,000 feet in about one hour. Most people who drive WILL experience varying degrees of altitude sickness (which will pass with time, medication, or simply descending). If you instead choose to climb Pike's Peak over a 2–3 day period, your prospects for altitude sickness sharply drop, and the severity of any symptoms also decreases. Over time, you adapt.

Both drinking at least 1–2 gallons of water per day and avoiding caffeine (found in coffee, tea, and chocolate) before and while ascending reduces the risk of altitude sickness. Interestingly, caffeine may alleviate symptoms once they begin. Alcohol increases the risk. Tobacco seems to increase the risk.

Avoid highly salted foods, which are dehydrating.

Ascending

Taking your time greatly reduces the risk of altitude sickness. Plan on taking at least 2 days to travel from sea level to 8,000 feet. After 8,000 feet, allow at least one day for each additional 2,000 feet of altitude. Schedule a rest day for every 2–3 climbing days after reaching 8,000 feet.

The mountaineer's step is recommended for ascending at altitude. It requires a short stride of 4–12 inches, a slow pace, and a weight shift from one foot to the other. This step enables you to naturally walk *poli - poli* and is the way to ascend while at altitude.

Remedies for Altitude Sickness

Descend. Descending even 500–1,000 feet may eliminate all symptoms. Resting for a day, or even a few hours at this level, may be sufficient for your continued journey.

Drink more water. Dehydration is a symptom of altitude sickness and exacerbates it. At higher altitudes, dehydration occurs more rapidly. More rapid breathing speeds dehydration.

Oxygen helps. If you have access to oxygen, try it. Increased oxygen helps prevent and reduce the symptoms of altitude sickness. Depending upon the severity of symptoms, oxygen can eliminate coughing, revive flagging energy, and stop a headache. It can enable you to sleep at night. It can rescue an otherwise failing vacation. Traveling in Tibet, where there is nowhere to descend except the southeast corner of the nation, a friend was miserable with coughing that kept her awake, nausea that kept her from eating, and a general malaise. Her tour group had flown to Lhasa, at a height of 13,000 feet, with no chance to acclimatize. She reported that her remedies (see below) helped (but not enough), and she was not scheduled to descend for another 72 hours. One dose of oxygen at her hotel, which she repeated 12 hours later, combined with natural remedies, did the trick. Her energy increased, her coughing ceased, and she resumed eating.

Homeopathic Remedies

Homeopaths recommend Coca 30c for the prevention and treatment of altitude sickness. (This is a specialty product; it will not get you high, and it does NOT contain cocaine!) Find homeopathic Coca on the Internet or contact a homeopath for further guidance. It works extremely well. In Gornergrat, Switzerland, altitude 10,000 feet, my climbing partner—normally a world class sleeper—could not sleep a wink. One pellet of Coca 30c beneath his tongue resulted in sound sleep within moments and also cleared his high altitude snoring. He needed and took another dose on 2 other nights with the same excellent results. I also have seen immediate reduction of rapid pulse and elimination of palpitations at high altitude from taking Coca 30c.

Hiking in the Rockies at above 13,000 feet, a friend who is prone to asthma ascended a peak and found herself wheezing heavily. Alone, she felt panic rising and her heart began to pound and ache. She pulled Coca 30c from her shirt pocket and took a dose. She felt immediate relief as her breathing slowed and her wheezing decreased. She repeated the dose 10 minutes later, and her symptoms ceased.

On a recent trip to Tibet, we flew from Beijing, China, altitude 144 feet, to Lhasa at 13,000 feet. Dizzy and queasy from the rapid increase in altitude, we gathered our gear at the airport, drove to our hotel, drank a lot of water, and turned in early. I could not sleep! I felt achy and sore from the trip and could not get comfortable. In the morning, having had very little sleep, my nose was congested and I found blood when I wiped it. My roommate's white pillow was stained red and her nose dripped blood. I took a dose of Arnica 6c and gave one to my roommate. My nose congestion cleared rapidly, and the blood was gone. I also felt less tired. My roommate's nosebleed slowed with 1 dose; we repeated the dose in 15 minutes and her nosebleed stopped. When she resumed bleeding about 30 minutes later, she took a third dose and the bleeding completely stopped.

Arnica is the perfect remedy for many types of trauma, especially when you feel bruised or achy. Yes, the bumps and jars of travel, carrying luggage, prolonged sitting, standing or walking, and changes in air pressure all create trauma. Arnica will slow or stop bleeding and hasten healing. It also is specific for insomnia with the feeling that the "bed is too hard" or that you "just can't get comfortable."

Prophylaxis

Prevention can be your best medicine. You CAN prepare for high altitude so that you reduce the possibility or severity of altitude sickness. Prepare at least 1-2 months in advance.

Exercise. Increase your fitness level before you travel to altitude—if you do, you will have less trouble breathing. Cardio is key. Walking, running, or using an elliptical machine improve your ability to breathe and use oxygen. The belief that you "cannot train for altitude" is only partially true and not very helpful! Though exercise at sea level will not reduce nausea at altitude, low fitness at sea level will leave you miserable at altitude. Train hard!

Build Your Blood. Once you arrive at high altitude, your body adapts by increasing your red blood cells, enabling you to better process oxygen. You can prepare in advance by optimizing your red blood count. One tablespoon of molasses, stirred into a cup of nettle leaf tea, taken twice daily will boost your blood. Snacking on a half cup daily of dried fruit, such as raisins, prunes, apricots, goji, longan, or mulberry will help. Eat bone soup 4 times per week. (Simmer 1 pound of large mammal (beef or bison) bones in 1 quart of water for 12 hours, add vegetables and herbs as desired, strain, refrigerate, skim the fat, reheat, season, and enjoy.) Consider the Chinese herbal formula, Dong Quai Four, also known as Si Wu Tang; take as directed. One or two months of blood building is optimal, but even a week prior to travel will help.

Hydrate. Three days prior to travel to altitude, focus on hydration. Drink plenty of water. I try for 6–8 cups daily. Continue hydration especially while traveling by air, in arid regions, and in sun or heat.

Avoid Dehydration. Avoid or reduce coffee, tea, and alcohol to a minimum because they are diuretics that drain fluids from the body. Dehydration aggravates altitude sickness and will worsen your headache. Plan to minimize bathing at altitude. Bathing reduces your natural body oils and allows more of your valuable fluids to escape.

Herbal Remedies. The Chinese have conducted extensive modern research into herbal remedies to prevent altitude sickness. They have focused on adaptogenic herbs, herbs that improve the body's ability to adapt to change and stress. These herbs include panax ginseng, tienchi ginseng, codonopsis, gynostemma, rhodiola, cordyceps, reishi mushroom, and schizandra. All of these work, singly or in combination. Excellent choices include Sheng Mai Yin, which contains panax ginseng, ophiopogonum, red sage root, and schizandra. Use as directed or take 3 grams twice daily of the dried herb or 1–2 droppers of tincture. Begin 3–7 days prior to travel and continue while at altitude.

Choosing Homeopathic Remedies

When shopping for homeopathic remedies, you will need to know both the name of the remedy and the potency. Obtaining the appropriate remedy is far more important than a particular potency. The potency is the number plus letter to the right of the remedy name on the label. I recommended 30c because that is the potency I use — it is generally available in my area, and it works well in first aid situations. If you cannot find 30c I recommend that you use potencies of 6x–30x or 6c–30c. A higher number indicates a higher potency.

Higher potencies are stronger than lower potencies, last longer, and require less frequent dosing. They typically are used for more serious issues.

I occasionally recommend remedies with the 200c potency, but the 30c potency will work! For example, Arnica 200c would relieve more of the pain and swelling of a sprained ankle, but lower potencies of Arnica would still be effective.

Sometimes you may see homeopathic combination remedies for sale. Combination remedies are blends of several homeopathic medicines that address a group of related symptoms. They are generally labeled according to their use. If a single remedy is not available, or you can't decide which single remedy would be most appropriate, choose the combination remedy intended for your ailment.

ALTITUDE SICKNESS

Dealing with High Altitude After You Arrive

Rhodiola. If I could carry only one herb with me to high altitude, it would be rhodiola. A plant that grows primarily at high altitude, *Rhodiola rosea* is an adaptogenic herb that builds energy, enhances immunity, promotes lung function, and increases endurance. It regulates the heartbeat and helps to prevent illness in cold and damp environments. I had been advised to try it, but was loath to set aside my tried and true altitude remedies. Trekking at above 15,000 feet in Tibet, the source for much high quality rhodiola, I took a single dose when suffering from altitude-induced headache and malaise. Immediately I could feel my lungs expanding and my headache easing. I was amazed at how much better I felt in just moments. I found that the tincture works well, 1 dropper in the mouth as needed, but that it works even better when added to a cup of hot water. Capsules of the dried herb work less quickly; to increase the speed and effectiveness, open the capsule and drop the contents into hot water. The hot water makes a major difference! A dropperful or a capsule is 1 dose. Take 1 dose every 30–60 minutes when suffering from altitude-caused distress, and then 3 times per day to support you at altitude. This herb is worth the expense and the space it takes up in your travel kit.

Ginkgo leaf. I highly recommend ginkgo leaf to both prevent and treat altitude sickness. I used it at up to 18,000 feet on Mt. Kilimanjaro and found it helpful, but not as helpful as rhodiola. Primarily known for increasing brain oxygenation and enhancing memory, ginkgo is effective, readily available, and extremely well tolerated. My physician friends like that they can find so much research demonstrating its value in preventing acute mountain sickness (AMS). (It also helps you to remember where you left your car keys!) As a preventative, I would take 1 dropperful of the tincture, 3 times per day, for 1–3 days immediately prior to climbing. It will reduce or eliminate the symptoms from ascending too rapidly. As a treatment, take 1 dropperful every 30–60 minutes. If symptoms do not improve, immediately descend at least 500–1,000 feet. **Caution: Ginkgo is a blood thinner; choose another herb if you take prescription blood thinners.**

Reishi mushroom. You may find this under the names ganoderma or ling zhi. Like coca leaf (see below), it has a long history of traditional mountain use. Reishi is an Asian mushroom (although closely related species are found in the United States) that also is used to treat cancer and allergies and as an immune stimulant. It also is used to promote spiritual wisdom and is one of the most revered herbs in the Chinese pharmacopeia. Traditional Chinese Medicine uses this herb specifically for asthma, coughing, insomnia, palpitations, dizziness, blood circulation, forgetfulness, and general debility. Not surprisingly, those are many of the symptoms of altitude sickness! The dose is 1 dropperful 3 times per day of the alcohol based tincture or 2 capsules 3 times per day to avoid altitude sickness. Take this dose hourly to treat altitude sickness. Reishi combines well with rhodiola and ginkgo.

Osha, a member of the ligusticum plant family, has been used traditionally by North American Indians for treating many respiratory problems, including pneumonia, bronchitis, asthma, and the common cold. They also use it to aid with breathing at high altitudes. While Indians chew a piece of the root to gain the benefits, you also can take osha tincture or capsules. The dose is 1 dropperful 3 times per day of the alcohol based tincture or 2 capsules 3 times per day to avoid altitude sickness. You can take this dose hourly to treat altitude sickness. Interestingly, osha typically grows at high altitudes.

ALTITUDE SICKNESS

Coca leaves. Yes, this is the source of cocaine and still is a key ingredient in Coca-Cola! (Coca-Cola enjoys an exemption from U.S. law that allows it to use specially processed coca leaf). Although individual possession or use of coca is prohibited in the United States, Canada, Great Britain, and other countries, you can legally possess and use it in Peru and Bolivia. Peruvian and Bolivian hotels serve coca tea. (Are you shocked? Cocaine is a highly refined product, but the plant's unrefined leaves are only a mild stimulant, similar in effect to coffee or black tea.) Peruvian travel guides commonly give the leaves to trekkers to avoid and treat altitude sickness. If you are taking coca and still experiencing altitude sickness symptoms, you likely are ascending too quickly. If offered coca in Peru, I would take it. Use like Peruvians do: chew on the leaves and drink the tea.

Altitude Sickness Summary

Avoidance is best.

- Drink plenty of water.
- Avoid heavily salted foods.
- Avoid caffeine.
- Avoid alcohol.
- When climbing above 8,000 feet, allow 1 day for each 1,000–2,000 feet additional altitude, and rest for 24 hours every 2–3 days.
- Prophylaxis:

  Herbs: Rhodiola, ginkgo, and/or reishi.

Treatment:

- Descend immediately at least 500–1,000 feet.
- Herbs:
  - Rhodiola.
  - Ginkgo.
  - Reishi mushroom.
  - Osha.
  - Coca leaf (where legal).
- Homeopathy: Coca 30c.
- Oxygen.

ALTITUDE SICKNESS

BITES & STINGS

I went hiking in the North Georgia mountains on a beautiful, perfect spring day. The dogwood trees were covered in white blossoms, and the hardwoods were filling out with fresh green leaves. The air was crisp, and you could smell the flowers. I lay down, still breathing hard from the climb, on a grassy hill. I felt the sun warming my face and the cool dampness of the grass. I heard birds in the distance and my companions close by. I felt at peace.

Someone called my name, and I turned my head. Suddenly, I felt a searing pain at my ear, a pain so severe and so sudden that I had trouble seeing. I called to my companions. They didn't understand that something terrible had just happened, and they continued laughing and talking. The pain consumed me — I hurt so badly that I could not think. I felt helpless.

An elderly local man came and offered assistance. As he helped me move into the shade and covered me with my jacket, he explained that I had been stung, probably by a bee.

"A bee caused this kind of pain?" I asked.

He told me that, depending where you are stung, the pain can be incredible. (It was!) He cautioned that although we would be able to numb the pain, it would continue for at least another 24–48 hours!

My new-found friend was right. We numbed the pain with a poultice made from a wad of chewing tobacco that we moistened with water and secured to my ear with a combination of Band-aids and duct tape. The pain immediately decreased!

I was amazed at how quickly the tobacco worked. My ear still throbbed but I could think again. When I touched the side of my face I could feel heat and swelling. Pressing an ice pack against my hot face provided temporary relief and gave me something to do. Aspirin helped slightly. When I removed the tobacco poultice much of the severe pain returned so I quickly replaced it. At home that night, I drank meadowsweet tea to reduce the pain and I slept with the tobacco poultice taped to my face. Towards the end of the second day the swelling and redness decreased. I awakened on the third day, pain-free!

BITES & STINGS

Bees, Wasps, Yellow Jackets, and Hornets

Avoid getting bitten. The proverbial ounce of prevention is worth the proverbial pound of cure. Be observant and cautious, and follow these simple tips to avoid bugs and their stings. Yellow jackets nest in dirt mounds, old logs, and dense shrubs. They also swarm at open food and open trash. When you're camping or picnicking, *cover your trash* and *don't leave food out*. Don't sit, eat, or rest near open trash or food. (Camp AWAY from the dumpster.) While it may be difficult to avoid all of these, be aware when you are poking around! According to the Centers for Disease Control and Prevention, 70 percent of all insect stings are from yellow jackets. Each yellow jacket is capable of multiple stings, so watch out.

When you are smelling the roses be aware of their other guests. Honeybees nest in hives, work around flowers, and often light on the ground to forage for food. The majority of bee stings are to the soles of bare feet! *Wear shoes* to avoid being bitten on your feet and ankles from stepping on a bee. When a bee stings you, the stinger stays with you and continues pumping venom into you long after the bee leaves. Remove the stinger immediately. See "Treatment for Insect Stings" later in this chapter.

Hornets and wasps nest in a variety of places, including on and under roofs, under eaves, and on the sides of buildings. They may nest in hollow places such as walls and abandoned beehives or in trees or shrubs. A football-shaped papery object hanging from a tree branch likely is a hornet or wasp nest. *If you see a nest, leave it alone.*

Insects may be sharing your drink or food without your knowledge! When outdoors, LOOK each time you pick up your drink or take a bite. Open sugary drinks attract stinging insects, especially yellow jackets. Careful — one may have crawled inside your open can of soda.

If a stinging insect is near you, remain calm. DO NOT move quickly or aggressively; move slowly. If you swat or flail about, a stinging insect may interpret this as aggression and sting you. If the insect lights on you, breathe deeply and wait for the insect to leave. Be patient.

Talk calmly to any insect that is buzzing around you or has lit on you. (Shouting "get away" at the top of your lungs does not qualify.) Encourage the insect to leave by telling it where to go for food and create a mental image of that place. Say something simple like, "Please leave. Go to the flowers up the hill." Repeat your encouragement and directions until the insect leaves. This really works. (OK, so you think this is entirely stupid. Try it anyway. If nothing else, it reduces your anxiety level by giving you something to do. Eventually, the insect will leave without having stung you, and you will feel like Dr. Doolittle.)

Do not smash a stinging insect. If it is a yellow jacket, smashing releases chemicals that alert fellow yellow jackets that war has been declared. DO NOT engage in warfare against stinging insects — you will lose.

Avoid looking or smelling like a flower! Bright colors and strong smells attract stinging insects. Entomologists tell us that yellow especially attracts, but that red does not. Flowery perfumes attract unwanted attention from stinging and biting insects — do not use them outdoors.

By the way, your insect repellent does NOT repel stinging insects! In fact, particularly smelly repellants may attract them.

Planning for Bee and Other Insect Stings

Stings from bees, wasps, hornets, and yellow jackets are unpleasant for everyone. At the least, you will experience a local response, which is restricted to the general location of the bite, and may include pain that lasts for several days, skin irritation, swelling, and a welt. Some people additionally experience a systemic, or whole body, response. If it is not local, it is systemic. A systemic response may include red skin far from the bite, welts, general skin itching, nausea, and headache, all of which may arise within moments of the bite. A small percentage of people, about 2 percent, experience a severe systemic response, which may include eye, lip, tongue, and throat swelling, hoarseness, trouble breathing, dizziness, and fainting.

All stings require immediate treatment. Severe systemic response, also called anaphylactic shock (when your throat closes up and you cannot breathe), requires immediate treatment plus medical attention.

You can die from a severe systemic response. Most deaths from bites occur within one hour of the bite. Once you have experienced a severe systemic response you are at risk for the same or worse response the next time you are bitten.

If you have experienced a severe systemic reaction or anaphylactic shock from bee or other insect stings, consider it your responsibility to carry your own emergency aid. I recommend that you *carry a bee sting kit,* that you learn how to use it, and that you keep the kit

BITES & STINGS

Creating Your Sting Kit
10 Helpful Items

1. Pen knife or expired credit card, for "flicking" out the stinger.

2. 2–3 epinephrine pens (syringes): from pharmacy with doctor's prescription.

3. Antihistamine:

Benadryl (diphenhydramine): from pharmacy, and/or osha herbal tincture: from herb store or herbalist.

4. Homeopathic remedies:

For bee stings: Apis 200c or 30c, from health food store or from a homeopath. Made from bees, this is the most specific of remedies for bee sting. It also works well for other insect stings and for jellyfish stings. Taken immediately, it can stop anaphylactic shock. It specifically reduces swelling and the pain of the sting. Take 1 pellet every 15–30 minutes for pain, every 5–10 minutes for throat swelling or difficulty breathing. If you know you're allergic, carry Apis 200c.

For wasp, yellow jacket, and hornet stings: Use Vespa 200c if you have it, Apis 200c if you do not. Use Vespa the same as you would use Apis.

For scorpion stings: Carry Androctonis (Scorpion) 200c or other scorpion remedies and use immediately as described above for bee stings.

For sea urchin stings: Scuba divers and snorkelers should pack Apis 30c and Silica 30c.

For jellyfish stings: Apis 30c, Ledum 30c, and Carbo veg. 30c are good choices.

See "Choosing Homeopathic Remedies," page 21.

5. Antiseptic:

2–3 alcohol wipes or echinacea tincture or tea tree oil or lavender essential oil.

6. 2–3 ice packs that cool when you break them: outdoors stores or pharmacy.

7. Topical pain killers:

Lavender essential oil: apply every 15–30 minutes (also calming and relaxing) or **Sting-Kill**: from pharmacy (contains benzocaine and menthol).

8. Internal pain killer (optional): Herbal: 4 droppersful of meadowsweet or willow bark tincture, every 15 minutes.

Pharmaceutical: Ibuprofen, aspirin, or acetaminophen.

9. Topical Antibiotic: Tea tree oil or lavender essential oil or triple antibiotic ointment.

10. Relaxant: Rescue Remedy flower essences or chamomile herb tincture or lavender essential oil.

readily available at all times — do not pack the kit at the bottom of your luggage! Do not rely upon your companions or even on local medical authorities for kits. Be prepared to take immediate action if you should get stung. If you cannot self-administer the kit, I recommend that you train someone in your group to assist you.

Kits include at least one, and preferably two or three, epinephrine pens (syringes), an antihistamine such as Benadryl, plus instructions. You can obtain epinephrine pens from your pharmacy with a doctor's prescription. While you are at the pharmacy, obtain an antihistamine. (Benadryl works very well but your doctor or pharmacist may recommend another drug or a stronger version of Benadryl). The immediate use of an epinephrine pen plus an antihistamine can save your life, especially when medical care is far away. Other helpful items for an insect sting kit are listed in "Creating Your Sting Kit."

Learn your options for treating insect stings and plan for them before you travel. Even a local response to a sting can ruin a trip. Carry a bee sting remedy with you.

Treatment for Insect Stings with Your Kit

Look for the stinger, which looks much like a tiny wooden splinter. If you see it, IMMEDIATELY *"flick" it out* with your fingernail, the edge of a knife, or a credit card. Do NOT pinch it out — you may force more venom into the skin! The stinger from some insects is a self-contained unit that continues pumping venom even though the insect has left. According to the CDC, even a 5-second delay can make a huge difference in the amount of venom that enters your system and the length of your recovery. Do NOT wait for the doctor.

31

Other Homeopathic Remedies for Stings
General Remedies Other than Apis

Vespa: Vespa 200c works even better than Apis for hornet, wasp, and yellow jacket stings. Apis and Vespa work best when the sting site is red, hot, and swollen.

Ledum: If the site is cool and perhaps purple, or simply if Apis and Vespa are not helping, use Ledum 200c. Ledum is perfect for many puncture wounds. Take as described above.

Hypericum: If the bite is on a finger or toe, I first would take Hypericum 30c or 200c; Hypericum is specific for finger and toe injuries (injuries to highly ennervated tissues). I have seen this work when the other remedies failed.

Special Tips for Spider Bites

Spider bites that are red and swollen respond well to Apis 200c taken every 15 minutes for 4 doses and then as needed to reduce pain and swelling.

If the spider is a black widow, or if there is high anxiety and especially if there are chills, take Arsenicum album 200c every 5–10 minutes. If there are cramps, take Belladonna 200c every 15–30 minutes.

If the spider is a brown recluse, the bite often will be on the hand. If on a finger, Hypericum 200c may provide superior relief to Apis. Use Anthracinum 30c, 4 times per day, internally and on the bite area, for the brown recluse bite, which is characterized by a red, white, and blue "bulls eye". Alternate Athracinum 30c with Apis 30c or 200c if the bite is hot and swollen, Hypericum 30c or 200c if the bite is on a finger or toe, and Ledum 30c or 200c if the bite area feels cool or cold.

If you know you are at risk of a severe systemic response, *use your epinephrine pen* NOW. Inject the syringe directly into your thigh. (You are at risk if you experienced a severe systemic response in the past and have not been de-sensitized to stings. Untreated, people become more sensitive over time.) Next, *take a dose of your antihistamine.* NOW call the doctor or begin travel to close-by medical attention.

If you are relying upon homeopathic remedies and herbs, take your first dose of Apis 200c NOW and repeat every 15–30 minutes for pain and swelling, every 5–10 minutes for throat swelling or difficulty breathing. Take Apis by placing 1 pellet beneath your tongue and letting it slowly dissolve. While it is dissolving, swallow 2 droppersful or approximately 40 drops of osha herbal tincture. Repeat osha as needed to improve your breathing. Apis specifically neutralizes the effect of the insect toxin and osha acts as a natural antihistamine. Apis works for bee, wasp, hornet, and other insect stings, and for a variety of other bites that create severe pain and anaphylaxis. For other homeopathic remedy suggestions, see "Other Homeopathic Remedies for Stings."

Wash the affected area with soap, water, and an antiseptic such as alcohol, tea tree oil, lavender essential oil, or echinacea tincture. This will reduce the risk of infection. You don't know where that stinger has been!

Apply ice directly to the sting site for 20 minutes to avoid and reduce swelling and to reduce pain. Continue to apply ice as needed. If the sting is to your leg or foot, elevate above the heart to reduce swelling and pain.

Topical pain-killers help. Apply 3–4 drops of Lavender essential oil directly to the sting — lavender is a natural anodyne (pain-killer) and anti-spasmodic, and it will help you to relax. Reapply every 15 minutes or whenever you feel the pain returning. Alternatively, look for Sting-Kill at your pharmacy. Sting-Kill contains benzocaine, which numbs the skin, and menthol, which reduces the itch. These remedies work surprisingly well!

Neutralize the venom. The venom from flying sting-ing insects is what causes the itching and pain. Soak a cotton ball in Echinacea tincture, tape it to the sting, and replace hourly — echinacea has strong anti-toxin qualities and will reduce the healing time. If you don't have Echinacea, you can neutralize the alkaline venom by using a weak acid such as apple cider vinegar. Baking soda, which is weakly alkaline, is a good choice if you have neither echinacea nor vinegar. Many physicians recommend cortisone or another steroid cream to reduce pain and itching.

Calm down! The more relaxed you are, the less pain you will feel! Breathe deeply. Take 4 drops of Rescue Remedy every 15 minutes. If you have lavender essential oil, put 1–3 drops on a cloth, bring it to your nose, and breathe deeply. Repeat as necessary. Alternatively, take a dropperful of chamomile tincture or a cup of strong chamomile tea every 30 minutes. Other helpful herbs include kava kava, passion flower, or valerian — take them the same as you would take chamomile but watch out — the valerian will make you sleepy!

Wilderness Treatment of Insect Stings

Follow the instructions above for treating stings.

Neutralize the sting by applying "the best" remedy — tobacco. Use chewing tobacco or pipe tobacco, or open a cigarette — any tobacco will work. Moisten with echinacea tincture, vinegar, water, or spit, and apply liberally to the sting. Tape or bandage this and change this dressing in 1–4 hours. Don't have tobacco? If you can locate it, *plantain leaf* works almost as well as tobacco. Pound the plantain leaf or rub it vigorously between your hands to break the cellular walls, moisten with echinacea tincture, vinegar, water, or spit, and apply the same as tobacco. Other alternatives include *wet mud, moistened clay,* or *moistened powdered charcoal.* Wet soil from a river or stream bed will work. The moistened mud, clay, or charcoal will draw out and neutralize the toxin. Apply the same way as tobacco.

Neutralize the alkaline venom of bees and wasps by applying your own spit directly to the sting — it is mildly acid. Did you bring any *aspirin* with you? Aspirin is acid — smash it to a powder, moisten, and apply to the sting. While you have the aspirin out, take 2 aspirins internally to reduce pain. If there are any willow trees close by, you can boil 2 tablespoons of the bark in 2 cups of water to make a tea to reduce your pain. Drink a half cup every 30 minutes. *Willow bark* contains salicylic acid, the primary ingredient in aspirin.

Apply ice or a cold pack if you have it. Using a cold compress — a cloth dipped in cold water — may ease discomfort.

BREATHE DEEPLY AND SLOWLY! Your anxiety level decreases with slowed and deeper breathing. Pain decreases as your anxiety level decreases. To further reduce anxiety, take 4 drops of Rescue Remedy beneath your tongue and sniff Lavender essential oil.

Desensitizing from Insect Stings

Anaphylactic shock is life-threatening, so it's no wonder the healthcare community has developed ways to desensitize susceptible individuals. Both allopathic physicians and homeopathic physicians, believing that "like cures like," use minute amounts of bees or bee venom to desensitize their patients. Allergists use allergy shots; homeopaths use sugar pellets that dissolve beneath the tongue. Does desensitization work? For most people, yes.

People who experience anaphylactic shock from stings and who commonly are exposed to stinging insects can obtain desensitizing shots from their doctor. Allergists find the shots to be 90–95 percent effective at eliminating the anaphylactic response. Typically, you

BITES & STINGS

would receive shots 2 times per week for 10–20 weeks, and then taper down to one shot every 1–2 months for a period of 5 years.

Homeopathy offers a similar strategy. Consult a professional homeopath for personal guidance, and review one of the excellent texts on homeopathy (see the Resources Section at the back of this book) for detailed descriptions of the underlying theory. To desensitize yourself, you would take one Apis 6c pill daily for 20–30 days. Cut back or stop if you begin experiencing any bee sting symptoms.

Planning for Insect Bites

I once took a summer-time bike trip along the barrier islands of North Carolina. I had been told that mosquitos were bad so I packed an insect repellant. We got out of our station wagon and into winds of 20 miles per hour. We unloaded the bikes, arranged our gear, and took off for Cape Hatteras. We rode peacefully for an hour, noticed that the wind had died down, and stopped to rest. Arrgh! There must have been thousands of mosquitos! Where had they come from? Our shorts and tank tops provided no protection. My friend must have had a hundred mosquitos just on one arm. They were in our eyes and we madly swatted at them. We jumped and yelled and scrambled to pull cans of spray repellant from the bikes. We took turns spraying each other and gradually began to breathe again.

Later, we learned that mosquitos in that area peak in late summer to early fall. Had we arrived in the spring, we might not have encountered any mosquitos. At the next store, we purchased additional repellant — just in case!

Avoiding Mosquito and Other Insect Bites

During the warm months in many parts of the world, biting insects are a fact of life. Mosquitos, gnats, biting flies, fleas, and ticks are common pests. If you will spend time outdoors, plan for bites.

Cover up. Long-sleeved shirts with cuffs, long pants with elastic cuffs, socks, and hats provide protection.

Oil up, naturally. A 50-50 combination of coconut oil with shea butter works amazingly well. It also helps prevent sunburn. Make your own, find it in a health food store, find it online, or ask your herbalist to prepare it for you. Neem oil may be mixed in to repel additional insects, including mosquitoes, flies, fleas, ticks, mites, and lice.

Chemical insect repellants work. Repellants containing DEET are very effective but may also be the most toxic. If you use them, especially on children, spray the clothes and not the skin. Do NOT spray pets with DEET! Remember, with pets and with small children, what goes on the pet or child goes in the pet or child. Wash your hands after using DEET. Another chemical repellant is Picaridin – it reportedly is effective and reportedly is less toxic than DEET. If you use it, follow the same safeguards you would use for DEET.

Natural insect repellants work. Available at health food stores and outdoors stores, these typically contain essential oils such as lemon eucalyptus, citronella, and lemongrass. Many are pleasant smelling and do not present the toxicity problems of chemical repellants. They are a great choice, especially in low to medium infestation areas or for short time periods. I use a combination of cedarwood, citronella, eucalyptus, and lavender essential oils. Make your own: In a 4 ounce spray bottle, place 5 milliliters (1 measuring teaspoon) essential oil(s), 15 milliliters (1 tablespoon) pure grain alcohol or vodka, and top off with 100 milliliters (about 3-1/2 ounces) of water. Shake well each time and spray.

BITES & STINGS

Eat lots of garlic. When you eat garlic, your skin exudes "eau de garlic." Mosquitos don't like the smell. (Unfortunately, your companions may not appreciate it either!)

Homeopathic. Try Staphasagria 6c before exposing yourself to mosquitos, then take one dose every 2–3 hours during exposure. Take as needed to reduce the itching of bites. Staphasagria will reduce the effect of bites in most people, but it doesn't help some people—especially heavy meat eaters. If it does not reduce the frequency of your mosquito bites, try Berberis 6c, taken as suggested above for Staphasagria. It can work where Staphasagria fails.

Don't eat sugar and cut back on fruits and fruit juices. Yes, eating sweets makes you smell sweet, especially to mosquitos. Perfume, scented deodorants, and after-shave also may increase your attractiveness to mosquitos.

Try a solar powered "mosquito guard." This device, which you wear on your belt or put in a pocket, emits a barely audible whine that discourages mosquitos. It's inexpensive and available from mail order catalogues. I have a mosquito-sensitive friend who swears by hers.

Avoid wearing blue. The color blue attracts mosquitos.

Treating Mosquito and Other Insect Bites

■ Immediate washing with soap and water will eliminate symptoms of many bites. Homeopathic Apis 30c or Ledum 30c will eliminate symptoms for many people. The dose is one pill every 15 minutes until the symptoms cease or moderate. The earlier you do this, the more effective the remedy. Arnica 30c, if you do not have Apis or Ledum, will reduce swelling.

- Lavender essential oil, applied directly to the bite, will reduce pain and swelling. The dose is 1–3 drops. This works for a wide range of bites, including mosquito and spider bites. Tea tree oil is a good second choice. Reapply whenever the pain or itching returns.

- Chickweed is one of the best herbal remedies for itching. You can find it growing wild in many temperate areas (especially in the lawn, at curbs, and at the sides of buildings). It also is widely available at health food stores. Pound and moisten fresh chickweed, or moisten dry chickweed, apply and tape to the bite, and replace every few hours. If you don't see any chickweed, plantain works almost as well. Or use one of the many excellent herbal salves containing chickweed.

- Ammonia or apple cider vinegar, applied directly to the bite, takes the sting and itch out of many bites. If one doesn't work, try the other. Ammonia works especially well on mosquito bites. After Bite, a drugstore product, uses ammonia as the active ingredient to eliminate mosquito bite itch. Baking soda mixed with water takes the sting out of many bites and is especially helpful with ant bites.

- Cortisone or other steroid creams relieve itch. Benadryl cream relieves itch.

- If bites result in a systemic response — that is, if your breathing becomes impaired or you develop red patches where you haven't been bitten — take internally an antihistamine such as osha herbal tincture or Benadryl. Seek medical attention for impaired breathing.

BITES & STINGS

Bites & Stings Summary

Avoid getting bitten:

- Be aware.
- Avoid nests.
- Cover food and drink.
- Wear shoes and socks. Cover up with long sleeves and pants.
- Remain calm. Move slowly. Do not swat or kill.
- Avoid bright colors (especially yellow and blue) and strong smells.
- Use repellants:

  Natural repellants: Lemon eucalyptus, citronella, and lemongrass essential oils. Coconut oil with shea butter and neem.

  Chemical repellants. **Caution**: DEET.

  Homeopathic: Staphysagria 6c.
- Eat garlic. Avoid sweets

Plan for stings and bites:

- Act quickly.
- If allergic, carry an epinephrine pen (by prescription only).
- Create a sting and bite kit — keep it handy.

Bites & Stings Summary continued

Treatment of insect stings and bites:
- Remove stinger.
- Anaphylaxis:

  Western medicine: Use epinephrine pen and take antihistamine.

  Holistic: Take homeopathic Apis 30c and osha root tincture.
- Wash with soap and water. Apply antiseptic (alcohol, tea tree oil, echinacea tincture).
- Ice. Elevate.
- Homeopathic: Apis 30c, Ledum 30c, or Arnica 30c.
- Herbs: Chickweed or plantain leaf.
- Pain and itch reduction: Lavender essential oil or Sting-Kill. (Or use vinegar, ammonia, baking soda, or a steroid cream or Benadryl.)
- Calm down. Breathe. Rescue Remedy. Lavender essential oil. Chamomile.

Wilderness treatment of insect stings:
- Tobacco. Mud, moistened clay, charcoal, spit, aspirin, willow bark, or plantain leaf.

Desensitizing treatments:
- Allergy shots.
- Homeopathy: Apis 6c.

BLEEDING

Twenty years ago I was in Cairnes, Australia taking a deep sea diving course so I could dive the Great Barrier Reef. Wow! I already had tickets for the dive boat and was planning to spend a week diving. On the third and final day of the dive course, as I was walking to the dive school, I cleared my throat and tasted blood. BLOOD? I never spit up blood! I was experiencing minor hemorrhaging from the water pressure. What could I do? If I continued to bleed, I would be DQ'd, disqualified, from diving!

I went searching for an herb to stop the bleeding. I looked first for comfrey, which grows wild. I knew comfrey to be one of the best anti-hemorrhaging agents — it would stop the bleeding fast. I was confident in my choice, but could not find the herb, either in the field or in the local herb shop. I also looked for cattails. Cattails, which grow in abundance in so many places, are great remedies for bleeding. Alas, they were not available.

Not knowing what else to do, I told my instructor who sent me to the school doctor. I asked, "Isn't there something [a drug] you can give me to stop the bleeding?" I thought to myself, this has to be a very common problem, surely he has something to solve it. The doctor shook his head. No. He pulled a paper from the stack on his desk, signed it, and handed it to me. The doctor had disqualified me. No! How disappointing! I could snorkel; I could not dive. Without the high water pressure from diving, my bleeding gradually stopped on its own. (I did go out on the dive boat and enjoyed snorkeling. The Great Barrier Reef really is worth it!)

I did not get to dive because I was not prepared. Years later, I was struck in the face by the hatch on a minivan. The hatch suddenly had flown upward, embedding my wire-rimmed glasses a quarter-inch into the bridge of my nose. Blood streamed down my face. I removed the glasses; the blood flowed faster. I washed the wound with soap and water, hoping the soap would stop the bleeding. It did not. The blood continued to flow.

This time I was prepared. I pulled a jar of a *comfrey-based salve* from my purse and pressed some into the cleaned wound. The bleeding stopped within 30 seconds! I stood looking at myself in the restroom mirror. Blood began seeping from my wound, I smeared on more salve and the bleeding ended. Despite the depth of the cut, my wound healed rapidly and without a scar.

A styptic pencil will stop bleeding from small cuts. (Ever watch boxing?) To stop bleeding from large cuts or wounds, Western medicine relies on coagulation products, cauterization, pressure, and surgery. Fortunately, we also have herbs and homeopathic remedies that stop bleeding.

Basic First Aid for Bleeding

When dealing with a bleeding cut, *applying firm pressure* to the wound, preferably with a clean cloth such as a T-shirt or scarf, may stop the bleeding. *Wash* the wound thoroughly with soap and water. This initial washing is critical, especially for puncture wounds, to reduce the risk of infection. Remember the old Western movies, where the doctor liberally poured whiskey into the wound? The whiskey served a double purpose: rinsing debris from the wound and killing bacteria in it.

Herbal First Aid for Bleeding

Herbs give you an additional tool to stop external and internal bleeding beyond the application of direct pressure. Hemostatic herbs (herbs that will stop bleeding) are widely available. *Yarrow* grows wild and is gaining popularity as a garden flower. Yarrow is my all-time favorite remedy to stop nosebleeds. Both dried

43

and fresh yarrow work well. Yarrow can be prepared as a tea: Add 2 tablespoons of the dried flowers and leaves to 1 cup recently boiled water and let steep 10–20 minutes. Of the tincture, take 1 dropperful every 10 minutes until bleeding stops.

I usually combine yarrow with *shepherd's purse.* Shepherd's purse, a common weed that I've seen growing at roadsides, at the edges of trails, in horse pastures, and at the edges of grassy fields, will stop internal and external bleeding. (It works well at reducing women's bleeding between cycles.) I recommend a tincture, given in the same dosage as yarrow. Although the fresh plant is considered superior to the dried, the dried will work in a pinch. Tinctures made from the fresh plant, available in health food stores, seem to work best. Take 1–4 droppersful hourly until the bleeding stops.

You can stop external bleeding by applying a hemostatic (stop bleeding) herbal tincture or salve directly to the wound—yarrow, shepherd's purse, comfrey, and tienchi ginseng all work well. Sprinkling *cayenne pepper* directly on the wound and holding it closed works well — alternatively, you could apply a poultice consisting of moistened fresh or dry herb to the wound. Poultices are easy to prepare and very effective.

Preparing a Poultice

To prepare a poultice, grind, rub, or pound 1–4 tablespoons of herb (to break the cell walls), moisten with tincture, tea, or pure water, place on plastic wrap or some other non-porous surface (even a Band-Aid), and apply directly to the wound. Secure in place with tape, a towel, a scarf, an elastic bandage, or whatever you have.

My favorite remedy to stop bleeding is *comfrey*. The botanical name is *Symphytum officinale*. It will stop hemorrhaging anywhere in the body (though Shepherd's purse and Tienchi ginseng are better for uterine bleeding) and works well with both internal and external bleeding. Comfrey taken internally will stop lung bleeding (coughing up blood), stomach bleeding (usually seen as black stool), and colon bleeding. Of course, you should see a healthcare provider to determine the cause of any of these conditions.

Comfrey in any form will work. Fresh or dried, leaf or root. It grows wild in many areas and is available in many health food stores in the United States and on the Internet. If it is unavailable in stores where you live and you do not have access to the Web, I suggest you grow your own. I think everyone should have a comfrey plant. It is easy to grow, quite hardy once it becomes established, and easily propagated from a piece of the root. (Caution: Comfrey can become invasive and dominate its area of the garden. Also, comfrey is tenacious — choose your location wisely because it will "insist" on returning even if you dig it up.)

One caution with comfrey when used externally— it can work too well! Not only will it stop the bleeding, but it will cause the tissue it touches immediately to begin healing. Really immediately. That means that you MUST thoroughly clean any wound prior to applying comfrey or you risk a nasty infection! It also means that you should NOT apply comfrey to a puncture wound — you run a major risk of abscess.

Why do I rate comfrey so highly? It is cheap, I've never seen a negative effect, and it works incredibly fast. It also will accelerate healing from any injury and from overexertion. It is my favorite post-surgical remedy. Formerly called "knitbone," it will greatly speed healing of (properly set!) broken bones. It will speed the mending of cracked ribs or of a sprained ankle.

BLEEDING

THE SAFE USE OF COMFREY

I and others consider comfrey an invaluable remedy that has been used safely for centuries by millions of people. Some authors criticize the internal use of comfrey due to the possible presence of pyrrolizidine alkaloids (PAs). If you choose to use comfrey and also choose to avoid the pyrrolizidine alkaloids: (a) only use comfrey that has the botanical name, *Symphytum officinale*: this species has lower PAs than other species and is the species that commonly grows in the United States; (b) only use comfrey leaf: the leaf has much lower PA levels than the root; and (c) consider using "pyrrolizidine free" comfrey preparations. *The Botanical Safety Handbook* by the American Herbal Products Association recommends that you limit (daily) internal consumption to 4 to 6 weeks per year and that you substitute other herbs if you have liver problems, are nursing, or are pregnant.

People use comfrey salves to speed healing for a wide variety of ailments. Do NOT use the salves on deep or puncture wounds unless those wounds have been thoroughly irrigated and cleaned. Comfrey works amazingly fast; the tissue that it touches first will heal first and debris trapped in a deep wound could cause infection. *The Botanical Safety Handbook* does not caution about PA content for the salves but advises that nursing mothers use other remedies for breast tenderness.

Oriental Herbs

I carry a vial of *Yunnan Paiyao* in my first aid kit to stop internal and external bleeding. Yunnan Paiyao is a Chinese "patent" medicine — a commercially available combination of herbs. The formulation has been kept secret for many years, although we know that the main ingredient is Tienchi ginseng. Tienchi ginseng stops bleeding, is anti-infective, reduces pain, and promotes faster healing. The Yunnan Paiyao vial contains an herbal powder topped by a tiny red pill.

Yunnan Paiyao may be taken internally (up to 3–4 doses per day) and the powder may be sprinkled directly on the wound. (I personally avoid placing anything in a wound, other than soap, water, or alcohol, unless the bleeding will not stop.) What about the tiny red pill? The pill is taken only for severe hemorrhaging, and is commonly used in the East by police for gunshot wounds. Yunnan Paiyao is inexpensive, easy to pack, and can be found in Oriental markets and Chinese herb shops.

Homeopathic Care for Bleeding

Arnica 30c is a fabulous remedy that I recommend you carry on all your travels. Yes, it can stop nosebleed. Yes, it likely would have stopped my lung bleeding at the Great Barrier Reef. Invaluable for any trauma, it will reduce bleeding and promote healing. All potencies will work. Follow the wound care recommendations above and take 1 pellet every 5–10 minutes to stop bleeding.

Phosphorus 30c is a great stop bleeding and anti-hemorrhaging remedy. If you don't have that with you, use *Ferrum Phos 30c*, which also will stop a cold if you take it immediately upon feeling symptoms.

Kitchen Remedies

Cayenne pepper will stop bleeding, both internally and externally. Not as powerful as comfrey or Tienchi ginseng, it is readily available from a kitchen, grocery store, or restaurant. For use on cuts, sprinkle directly into the cut, hold the edges of the cut closed for 2–5 minutes, and breathe calmly as you wait for the bleeding to stop. Your blood forms a paste with the cayenne that stops the bleeding. Re-apply as necessary. Alternatively, make a paste by combining about a 1/4 teaspoon of water with a teaspoon of cayenne and apply that paste to the cut. Interestingly, most people find that it does not sting on a simple cut but it will sting on a scrape. Plan to wash the cayenne off after the paste dries and a clot has formed - cayenne can blister your skin if left on too long. Mixing a teaspoon of cayenne into a half cup of water and drinking it will slow and even stop bleeding. It also will warm you! Uncooked, it will not create the burn you experience with spicy foods. This is one of the very best kitchen remedies and is easy to carry in capsules.

Black pepper, ground. Use as described above for cayenne.

Sage. Another spice rack remedy, sage leaves are wonderfully astringent and antiseptic. Mix a little water with a teaspoon or more of sage and apply this paste to the bleeding cut. Or apply dry sage directly to the wound and apply pressure.

Speaking of kitchen remedies, if nothing else is available, try *vinegar*. Take a teaspoon of vinegar every 15 minutes until the bleeding stops. I think of vinegar as a great emergency remedy for nosebleed or spitting up blood. You can find vinegar in kitchens, restaurants, and food stores around the world.

When all else fails or if nothing else is at hand, use *ashes*. Ashes? Yes. Ashes are one of the BEST ways to stop external bleeding. The Chinese traditionally use the ash from moxa — which is made from mugwort — by sprinkling it into the wound. You can use ashes from burnt wood or even from burning your own hair! Why is this remedy listed last? Because it WILL cause tattooing (skin discoloration) that will persist for some time.

Western Remedies

Styptic Pen. Carry a styptic pen to stop small bleeding problems. Available inexpensively in the shaving section of many Western pharmacies, a styptic pen combines astringents such as aluminum sulfate with a binder. It works by astringing the tissues surrounding a bleed, thereby stopping the flow of blood. To use, wash the cut with soap and water, rinse away the blood, and apply and dab the moistened tip of the styptic pen in the cut until the bleeding stops.

Hemostatics. One new product, QuikClot, is amazingly effective. QuikClot is used extensively by the military and by urgent care providers (emergency rooms and emergency medical technicians) and stops minor to severe bleeding. Applied externally, it can stop a nosebleed, arterial bleeding, or oozing from a scrape. The active ingredient in QuikClot is the mineral Zeolite, which greatly accelerates blood coagulation. QuikClot is available to consumers as a Zeolite-infused gauze that is pressed directly to a bleeding wound. Find this in pharmacies or online. I highly recommend that you include this in your first aid kit, especially if you are traveling to remote areas. This is a life saver. I recommend QuikClot for severe bleeding, but I do NOT recommend it for minor cuts—use pressure and less expensive remedies for minor cuts.

There are other hemostatics available in pharmacies. **Caution: If you are allergic to shellfish, do NOT use a hemostatic containing Chitosan.**

49

Bleeding in the Wilderness

As a child, I wanted to know what plant or what tree you could use to stop bleeding. What if my friends and I were stuck in the woods (which were adjacent to our backyard!) and Johnny fell, struck his head on a sharp stone, and began bleeding to death? What would we DO? (Home was only 50 yards away, but what if?)

I decided to learn which plants stop bleeding. The *Junior Girl Scout Handbook* was no help; the *Boy Scout Handbook* also had no information on hemostatic (stop bleeding) herbs. I asked every adult who I thought should know what I thought was basic and life-saving information. I asked medical doctors, nurses, and veterinarians. None of them knew.

Over the years, I learned that some people did know. I met naturalists, park rangers, and Native Americans who knew emergency wilderness medicine and knew how to use plants to stop bleeding. I was surprised to learn that many herbs that stop bleeding are easily identified shrubs and trees. Later, I found extensive documentation supporting this use of plants, and I saw plants stop bleeding. I highly recommend that wilderness hikers learn to identify at least a few of the plants that stop bleeding. As an added bonus, most of these plants also stop diarrhea! (Obtain a good field guide that illustrates and describes medicinal plants in your area. Depending where I am, I hike with *A Field Guide to Medicinal Plants and Herbs of Eastern and Central North America* (Peterson Field Guides) by Steven Foster and James A. Duke or *Medicinal Plants of the Mountain West* by Michael Moore. You can find field guides for most areas in the world.)

Cattail pollen, from the brown fuzzy spike that grows along roadsides, in swamps and alongside streams and ponds, is an excellent remedy to stop both internal and external bleeding. To use, shake the brown

50

and fuzzy part in a bag or cloth and collect the yellow pollen. Place the pollen on the bleeding area. Bleeding will immediately slow. For severe hemorrhaging, mound up the pollen on the cut and secure with a bandage or clean cloth. Stirring a teaspoon of the pollen into water and drinking it will reduce bleeding from the inside. Roasting the pollen first will increase the potency. Roast it by heating in a dry skillet until the pollen begins to brown, and then remove from heat. I especially like cattail pollen as a wilderness remedy because it is so easily identified. The ONLY drawback to cattail pollen is that many states in the United States prohibit gathering it. (It DID grow in the woods behind our house.)

Comfrey, mentioned above, is an outstanding remedy to stop bleeding. Simply pressing the leaves on the wound will stop bleeding. Bruising the leaves by pounding or rubbing them will increase the effectiveness. Can't find any? Try to find one of the other remedies on this list.

Yarrow, a common garden and wildflower, is another great choice. I would use the leaves. Bruise the leaves and press directly on the wound. A tea made from a quarter cup of the flowers and leaves simmered for 10–20 minutes in a cup of water will slow both internal and external bleeding. It also slows diarrhea. (It is one of my favorite remedies. When you begin coming down with a cold, try sipping a half cup of the tea every hour.)

Plantain is a very common roadside and trailside plant that grows prolifically throughout temperate regions. It's nicknamed "white man's foot" because it is most commonly found in high traffic and disturbed areas. Both the narrow (lance) leaf and round (broad) leaf varieties slow bleeding. Use the leaf to slow bleeding and also to fight infection. Used externally, the crushed fresh leaf kills bacteria and slows bleeding. Use it to heal trauma, open sores, and bleeding wounds.

BLEEDING

Taken internally as a tea, it helps to fight infection and even will help to clear urinary tract infections.

The leaf and root of *wild blackberry, wild raspberry,* and *wild strawberry* plants all slow bleeding and diarrhea. The root is stronger than the leaf; use the root to make tea while pressing the well-bruised leaf against the wound. The leaf tea is also a tasty beverage. Simmer a quarter cup of leaf in 2 cups of water for 20–30 minutes and drink a half cup every 15–30 minutes.

Having trouble recognizing the small plants? The mighty *oak tree* — easy to recognize by its acorns — helps to stop bleeding. Although it may not work as quickly as cattail, comfrey, or yarrow, it will work. Prune a small branch, strip off the outer bark and use the inner bark to make a poultice. Simmer 2 tablespoons of the bark in 2 cups of water for 20 minutes and sip to stop internal bleeding or diarrhea. Can't wait? Use the leaves to make a poultice while waiting for the bark preparation. The white oak is considered the best of the oaks therapeutically, but I will happily use the oak that I find.

Ailanthus, the star of *A Tree Grows in Brooklyn*, is native to the Orient but grows in urban and rural areas throughout the United States. Also known as Chinese sumac, ailanthus is famous for growing where no other tree can — out of cracks in the sidewalk, in building foundations, and at the edges of fields and streams. One day I was with students harvesting ailanthus bark when one student accidently cut deeply into her palm with her knife. She calmly walked over to me with ailanthus bark in one hand and a growing pool of blood in the other, looked me straight in the eyes and said, "Fix me, please." I asked that she press a strip of bark onto her wound while another student prepared to tie it into place with a bandanna. Of course, everyone was excited to apply a natural remedy in a wilderness setting! Within moments, the bleeding stopped. Back at school, we removed the bark, washed the cut with soap and water, applied alcohol, and bandaged with a fresh strip of ailanthus and a pharmacy dressing. The next day, the cut was healing nicely and the dressing was replaced with a simple bandage. Success!

Spider web. This is a GREAT remedy to stop bleeding! Found indoors or out, gather spider "silk" by wrapping it around one or two fingers, then apply directly to the wound. No, it is not clean and it is not pretty. But it is fast and effective.

In an emergency, if I could find nothing else, I would use clean *campfire ashes* or *ashes from burned human hair*. I would accept the temporary tattooing in return for saving a life.

BLEEDING

Bleeding Summary

Top choices of "packable" bleeding remedies (you only need one):
- Yunnan Paiyao vials.
- Comfrey tincture or capsules.
- Yarrow tincture.
- QuikClot hemostatic gauze.

Herbals:
- Yarrow
- Shepherd's purse.
- Comfrey.
- Tienchi ginseng tincture, powder, or capsules.

Kitchen remedies:
- Cayenne or ground black pepper.
- Sage leaf.
- Vinegar.

Pharmaceutical remedies:
- Styptic pen.
- QuikClot gauze.

Top choices for wilderness bleeding remedies:
- Cattail pollen.
- Yarrow leaves and flowers.
- Plantain leaf.
- Blackberry, raspberry, and strawberry leaf and root.
- White oak inner bark.
- Ailanthus inner bark.
- Spider web.
- Ashes.

BLISTERS

As a traveler, martial artist, and athlete, I have had my share of blisters. There are so many blister stories to tell! Still, one stands out.

My roommate and I were new students at Marlboro College in Vermont. We were looking forward to the weekend — she would travel to Bear Mountain for a hiking trip and I planned to participate in on-campus activities. On Friday afternoon she walked into our room, exuberant, carrying a large box. We plopped onto her bed. She opened the box and pulled out a brand new pair of heavy duty all-leather Dunham hiking boots. They were great! We admired them. They were the ultimate in style for a school obsessed with the outdoors.

My roommate had a choice: She could wear her old, ratty, stained, scuffed, and comfortable boots or she could wear her brand new all-leather Dunham hiking boots with the trendy Vibram lug soles. It did not take long to decide. After all, this was to be a short hike. She was going to climb Bear Mountain, camp at the top, and climb down the next day. She knew that hiking boots required a breaking-in period; she decided to break them in on the hike.

My roommate wasn't looking for advice.

On Saturday she pulled on heavy hiking socks but had trouble lacing her boots, so she changed to a thin pair of socks that also matched her shorts. These socks were dirty, so she quickly washed them and dried them as well as she could by rolling them in a towel. "I'll be fine," she said as she ran for the waiting car.

She looked great.

The hike was longer and more challenging than anyone had imagined, and I heard those socks stayed wet all the way to the top of Bear Mountain. (Did I forget to say it was freezing and that no one had planned

55

BLISTERS

for cold?) My roommate reported that her feet ached on the way up. The boots pinched in some places, rubbed in others, and just generally felt hard. But walking up was nothing compared to walking down! Her feet burned all the way. She felt her feet sliding forward in her boots. She feared she was shredding her feet but was too embarrassed to complain or ask for help.

My roommate limped into our dorm room on Sunday night. We closed the door, and I helped her to her bed. Gingerly, I helped pull off her boots and peeled off her socks. What a sight! Her feet were damp, wrinkled, and scattered with Band-aids. Some Band-aids appeared to have shifted, judging from the gray Band-aid glue on much of her skin. Many spots were red. The top layer of skin had begun separating from her feet, and the skin was filled with fluid. Blisters had formed. Blisters beneath Band-aids were intact, but most of the other blisters had torn. We gently washed her feet and sprayed them with Bactine. She wore sandals for the next few days. I became interested in blisters.

Those of us who wear brand new shoes for long journeys ought to plan for blisters. Blisters happen. They also happen to folks who DO break in their footgear but are not accustomed to the intensity of their journeys.

What Are Hot Spots and Blisters?

Hot spots are painful, red areas on the skin surface that have been caused by friction. If the friction continues, hot spots become blisters.

Blisters are raised, fluid-filled bubbles of skin. Blisters typically are caused by friction or by intense or prolonged heat. They actually are a separation of the layers of skin. Blisters may be filled with blood, in which case they are called blood blisters or hematomas. Blisters may be small or large. Blisters easily may range from one centimeter in diameter to large (50 centimeter) coin-sized blisters that cover the feet (or any other exposed skin).

Blisters can ruin an otherwise wonderful trip. They can be surprisingly painful and may engage all of your attention. Blisters may physically prevent you from wearing certain shoes because of swelling, bleeding, oozing, or pain. Blisters can stop you from sightseeing, trekking, or even going to dinner. Infection may additionally complicate blisters.

Avoiding Hot Spots and Blisters

To avoid hot spots and blisters, *stay dry* and *reduce chafing*. As a general rule, get a good fit with all of your gear. Anything that rubs against your body for a long enough period of time will cause hot spots and blisters. *Cornstarch* absorbs moisture and reduces chafing, and *powdered slippery elm bark* or *marshmallow root* provide additional relief. Many athletes use *tape* or *moleskin* directly on the skin where they know friction occurs. Athletes commonly tape their feet and hands. *Specialty fabrics* (such as CoolMax) that wick moisture away from the skin will keep you drier than most other fabrics.

Bar soap can prevent blisters and hot spots. "Soap your socks" by turning a sock inside out, placing it on your hand, scrub the sock with a lightly moistened bar of soap, allow to dry, and turn right side out. Repeat with the other sock. This works extremely well.

Wear dry and clean socks. Change and wash your socks daily, more frequently if you feel hot spots developing.

For *walkers, hikers, and runners*, wearing good-fitting shoes is a must. Shoes that are too tight or too loose WILL result in hot spots and blisters. DON'T purchase shoes that are a half size too large or too small, just because they are on sale. For long hikes and treks, plan on wearing two pairs of socks — a thin inner pair (silk is a good choice) and a thicker outer pair to reduce friction. When you purchase hiking and trekking boots, size them while wearing both pairs of socks. Many specialty shops and mail-order providers sell silk socks and glove liners. Many trekkers prefer single socks with double-layer soles.

Cyclists, you need to take the time to find gloves, shoes, and a seat that fits YOUR body. Blisters around the groin and buttocks are no laughing matter — and they are common. Many cyclists wear padded cycling pants or cycling pants with a chamois or synthetic chamois crotch — these reduce friction and provide an extra layer between you and the bike. Again, cornstarch is very helpful; apply liberally. (Ladies, no talcum powder here, please!) If your hands blister, even with gloves, consider padded handlebar tape. Also, have you and your bike checked for proper fit. A few minor adjustments to your bike could increase your comfort level significantly.

For *travelers carrying or dragging bags*, adjust all straps to provide the best fit for you. If the straps or handles still cut into or rub against you, pad them or buy replacement straps from a luggage shop. Also, consider strengthening or reinforcing your skin with additional clothing, Band-aids, or tape. Wear gloves.

Travelers may "toughen" feet and hands prone to blisters by soaking them in cold *black tea* or by applying moistened black tea bags. The tannins in the tea strengthen the skin and reduce the likelihood of blisters. Tea made by simmering a strip of *oak bark* (which also contains tannic acid) in 2 cups of water also will strengthen the skin.

Treating Hot Spots and Blisters

Treat hot spots or blisters immediately! Quick action may enable you to avoid a blister or eliminate one that has already begun. Even tough guys get blisters—treating yours immediately will save you time and discomfort down the road.

Soothing herbal salves and oils speed recovery from hot spots. A single drop of *lavender essential oil*, rubbed into a hot spot, may eliminate it by morning. Other excellent herbal solutions include *St. John's Wort* oil, salve, or tincture; *calendula* oil, salve, or tincture; or *comfrey* oil, salve, or tincture. When possible, leave the hot spot uncovered and exposed to the air until you are ready to resume your activity.

Soak your feet. To 2 cups of warm water, add 1 strip (½ ounce) of willow bark, ½ ounce grated, minced or powdered ginger, or a half cup of Epsom salts. Add a few drops of Lavender essential oil if you have it. Dissolve 1 pellet of homeopathic Arnica 30c or 1 pellet of homeopathic Ferrum Phos 30c to further boost the anti-inflammatory effects. Stir thoroughly. Soak your feet 15–20 minutes, remove them, and dry. This foot soak relieves discomfort and promotes healing. Add black tea or oak bark to the soak to help toughen the skin.

A freshly cut *raw onion*, rubbed on your hot spots and sore skin, may eliminate the hot spots by morning.

When you are ready to resume your activity, cover any hot spots. A simple Band-aid may be sufficient. First aid tape works well. (Even duct tape works when you have no other tape available.) *Self-adhesive moleskin* is an excellent choice. If the hot spot is small, cut a hole in the center of some moleskin a little larger than the hot spot and position over the hot spot. Alternatively, place some cotton or gauze over the hot spot and cover with a larger piece of moleskin. *New Skin*, a liquid

59

preparation that dries on contact, provides an additional layer of "skin." It does work, although debates continue as to whether it is superior to other methods. A product called 2nd Skin is positioned directly over the hot spot and taped into place. Some wilderness medicine physicians recommend it.

Blisters present more difficulties than hot spots. Apply a drop of *lavender essential oil* directly to the blister. This will reduce any pain, reduce the likelihood of infection, and accelerate healing. Tearing or puncturing a blister increases the risk of infection, so avoid this when possible. If you must puncture a blister, for example, if the blister is large, painful, and prevents necessary walking, do what you can to reduce the risk of infection.

To *puncture and dress a blister:*

1. Gently wash the blistered area with soap and clean water. Pat or air dry.

2. Sterilize a needle or tip of a knife by holding it in a flame. Wipe the needle or knife clean with a cloth moistened with alcohol.

3. Pierce the edge of the blister, inserting the needle or knife tip just far enough to express fluid from the blister.

4. Gently press the blister to release the fluid.

5. Apply a drop of lavender essential oil, tea tree oil, iodine, echinacea tincture, alcohol, or antibiotic ointment directly to the opening.

6. Position Second Skin or another commercial dressing directly over the blister and tape into place. Alternatively, use a Band-aid.

To continue treating a blister:

1. Additional tape will reduce friction. Be sure to eliminate all wrinkles in the tape and bandage. The wrinkles also create blisters.

2. When possible, change the dressing daily and reapply an essential oil (tea tree or lavender), echinacea tincture, or antibiotic ointment.

3. When possible, air dry the blistered area daily, preferably for four or more hours. If the blister is torn, apply an essential oil (tea tree or lavender) or echinacea tincture, and coat the skin with a comfrey herbal salve or an antibiotic ointment.

Homeopathy

My favorite remedies for blisters are Rhus tox, Nat mur, and Arnica. Choose Rhus tox if you are stiff or sore from over-exertion or if you feel better moving. Choose Nat mur if you just want to be left alone and reject assistance from others. Choose Arnica if you cannot get comfortable or if you feel sore or bruised. If you only have one remedy, try that one! Take 1 pellet every 15 minutes for a total of 4 doses and then take 1 pellet every 2 hours for the 30c potency. If you are using the 200c potency take 1 pellet every 4–6 hours.

BLISTERS

Blisters Summary

Avoid blisters:

- Keep high friction areas dry.
- Good fitting shoes and gear.
- Use powder to absorb moisture and reduce chafing: Cornstarch *and* slippery elm bark *or* marshmallow root.
- Use moleskin or tape.
- Soap your socks.
- Wear 2 pairs of socks.

Treating hot spots and blisters:

- Get immediate treatment — do not delay.
- Use herbal salves and oils to speed recovery: Lavender essential oil *or* St. John's wort, calendula, or comfrey oil, salve, or tincture.
- Expose to air when resting, cover when active. Band-Aid, first aid tape, moleskin, New Skin, or 2nd Skin.
- Apply an antiseptic to open blisters: Lavender essential oil or tea tree oil *or* echinacea tincture *or* iodine or alcohol *or* antibiotic ointment.
- Change the dressing on open blisters daily.
- Homeopathic remedies help:
  Nat mur.
  Rhus tox.
  Arnica.

BURNS

I was eating dinner in a Mongolian guesthouse at least 200 miles from the capital city of Ulaanbaatar when the owner rushed over to me. Through our interpreter, she asked if I could come quickly to the kitchen. I grabbed my remedy kit and followed her. The kitchen was filled with steam, a huge stove and oven, five adults all explaining in their language what had happened, and one very small young boy. The boy, who looked to be about 7 years old, sat on a high stool and extended his hand to me. His palm was very dirty and badly burned and he pointed sadly to a large metal skillet with a metal handle.

His palm it was red and beginning to blister. This had to hurt! The boy did not cry and instead looked very brave. The owner pointed to the boy and to herself — this was her son! She nodded her head at me, at her son, and at my kit.

I gently washed his palm with soap and water. Taking a bottle of lavender essential oil, I applied drops of the oil directly to the entire burn area. The boy's sigh told me that it already was reducing his pain. Looking at the remedies in my homeopathic kit, I considered Cantharis, which is so good for burns, but I decided to use Nat mur 200c for this special boy. Nat mur is useful for burns and blisters, especially for responsible or stoic people who hold back their tears when others would cry. I placed a pellet beneath his tongue. He closed his eyes, leaned backwards and tears began to flow. I turned to his worried Mom, clapped my hands, and said, "Good, good." The boy opened his eyes wide, held up his hand, and smiled at it and at me. No pain! I bandaged his hand, gave the mom 3 additional Nat mur pellets, and instructed her to give one per day to her son.

Two days later I saw the boy. He had lost the bandage I placed on his hand! I examined his palm and saw only slight redness and no blistering. He smiled and returned to the kitchen — he had work to do!

About Burns

Burns result from too much heat, including sunburn and scalding from boiling water, hot oil, electricity, or touching a hot surface. Burns often become blisters. They can be painful, can result in loss of skin, and can become infected if there is loss or penetration of skin. Burns can linger, taking a long time to heal.

Immediate appropriate response to burns can greatly reduce skin damage and reduce the risk of blistering. Sometimes, taking immediate and appropriate action will completely eliminate any pain or other sign of a burn. Act immediately. As a general rule, seek assistance if the skin is charred or if the burned area is open and more than 3 inches in diameter.

Treating Burns

Homeopaths recommend that you gently warm burned skin by immersing in hot water. (Actually, warmed alcohol is preferred but is not as easily obtained when traveling.) Warming the skin initially will increase the pain, but the pain quickly will subside. If immersion is impractical, cloths dipped in hot water (or warmed alcohol) also may be used. Keep moistening the cloths until the pain subsides. (The water should be hot enough that an unburned hand would perceive it as hot but not unbearable.) No liquids available? The burned area may be held close to a smoldering coal, lighted cigarette, moxa stick, or even the flame of a candle. Again, the key is to use heat that is hot but not unbearable to an un-burned hand. Continue the warming treatment until the pain goes away.

Thinking of using cold water instead? I've used both cold and hot methods. Cold provided immediate relief, but the pain returned immediately upon withdrawal and I was left with a significant burn! Alternatively, heat provides a brief increase followed by a rapid decrease in pain, no increase in pain upon withdrawal, and scant or no evidence of a burn. I am very clear that I will use heat the next time I burn myself!

Clean the burn area. Especially if the skin is broken, use soap and water (or an antiseptic solution) to clean the burn, and remove any debris from the wound to reduce the risk of infection. Continue cleaning the burn area two times daily while the skin is broken.

Apply a topical remedy. Topical burn remedies are used to prevent the risk of infection and to hasten healing.

Apply a dressing. Apply gauze or a fresh clean cloth, loosely, to protect the burn. Plan to change this at least 2 times per day.

Topical Remedies

At home, I always have an *aloe vera* plant growing in my kitchen. Aloe is inexpensive, very easy to grow, and almost impossible to kill. You say you just grabbed a dish from the oven without a pot holder? You accidently spilled boiling water that burned your hand? You lifted opened a steaming fish en papillote and the steam burned your finger? Tear off an inch of the leaf, more for large areas, split in half with a fingernail or a knife and apply the leaf or its gel directly to the burn. This is a fabulous burn remedy that will accelerate healing of damaged skin. Carry bottled aloe gel with you for sunburn and other burns. Aloe gel is available in many pharmacies especially during spring and summer months, in natural food stores, in large supermarkets and online. Aloe leaf is available at some farmers markets and is widely available in many sub-tropical and tropical areas. The plants are available in plant stores and grow wild in many areas.

Calendula herbal tincture, diluted with 1 part calendula tincture to 1–2 parts pure water, is a wonderful topical for burns. It helps to clear germs from the area, promotes skin healing, and has a long history of use for burns. *Plantain leaf* or *witch hazel* herbal tincture, diluted as above, work almost as well as calendula. See the "Herbs for Burns" for how to make an herbal burn tea.

Honey, applied full strength to the burn, is antiseptic, hastens healing and has a long history of use for healing burns. Find this in kitchens, restaurants, natural food stores, and food markets. Any 100% honey will work — avoid honey that has been combined with corn syrup.

Mustard is one of my favorite burn remedies. Use prepared mustard (the kind you would use on hot dogs and hamburgers); any variety will work. Apply directly to the burn area, but rinse with water after about 5 minutes. Re-apply as needed. I have used mustard for burns in the kitchen and at the grill and it never fails to work. Carry a mustard condiment packet for emergencies!

Lavender essential oil is a must for your travel kit and is invaluable for burns. Applied immediately, it helps to avoid blistering. It accelerates skin healing, is antiseptic, and relieves pain. Apply to the burn and breathe deeply — the scent of lavender relieves shock. Use 1 drop of essential oil for every square inch of burn. Apply directly to the burn, straight from the bottle, or spray from a bottle in a water base. *Helichrysum essential oil* may work as well or better.

If I did not have any of the above topical remedies, I would gladly apply an *antibiotic ointment* to broken skin from a burn. Widely available in pharmacies and online, I recommend that everyone carry this in their travel kit.

Homeopathy

My favorite homeopathic burn remedy is *Cantharis* 30c. When burned, immediately dissolve one pellet beneath your tongue. Repeat every 15 minutes for the initial pain and then 2–3 times per day. If you do not have one of the topical remedies listed above, you can make your own! To treat the skin topically, dissolve a pellet in 8 ounces of water (crush it first or stir the pellet in water rapidly) and apply the Cantharis water directly to the burn. Repeat every 15 minutes for an hour or until the pain subsides; repeat when the pain returns. If the pain wakes you up, take 1 pellet hourly, inserting the pellet between the gum and the lip. This remedy also will help heal an older burn, but it is spectacular when used immediately on fresh burns. Cantharis also relieves many burning bladder and urinary tract infections. If you don't have Cantharis, substitute homeopathic *Causticum* 30c or homeopathic *Urtica urens* 30c.

Arsenicum 30c is the remedy, even better than the above, if the person is very anxious. It also is the top choice if the skin is charred — in this case, take 1 pellet every 15 minutes during the first hour while seeking medical assistance. For a burn with charred skin, take Arsenicum 200c if you have it. Continue with this remedy hourly as needed.

Natrum muriaticum (Nat mur) 30c is a wonderful remedy for sunburn or sun poisoning and for burns with blisters. It is perfect for people who endure their burn despite the pain. Take 1 pellet beneath the tongue before, during, or after sun exposure. It helps not only with the burn but also with dehydration. *Belladonna*

30c is another great sunburn remedy, especially if you are red or feeling feverish.

Use homeopathic **Arnica** 30c or **Aconite** 30c for shock. Useful for so many traumas, Arnica will help clear shock that commonly results from burns. Take 1 pellet beneath the tongue. I would take this 1 or 2 moments AFTER the first dose of Cantharis (or other remedy listed above).

Homeopathic care can be used exclusively for small and minor burns. If there is blistering or a large area is involved, plan to include an herbal lotion to moisten the skin, relieve inflammation, promote healing, and relieve pain.

Herbs for Burns

Herbs can be used alone or, more effectively, in conjunction with other remedies. Herbal teas or lotions keep burned skin hydrated, especially useful when the burn covers a large area. *Calendula* is my favorite, but *plantain leaf, witch hazel, nettle leaf,* and *St. John's wort* all work well. Make the burn tea by simmering an ounce of herb in 1 pint of water for 20–30 minutes. Strain and cool. Use the cooled tea to keep a burn dressing moist, or use it as a cooling wash on the burn. Alternatively, make an herbal lotion by adding 1/2 teaspoon (2.5 ml) of the one of the above tinctures to 1 cup of pure water. Use it externally the same way you would use the herbal tea.

Burns Summary

Cool the burn to stop damage.
- Gently warm the burned skin.
- Clean with soap and water or antiseptic wash.

Topical remedies to reduce infection and hasten healing:
- Aloe gel: from bottle or plant leaf.
- Calendula, plantain, or witch hazel tincture, half strength.
- Honey.
- Prepared mustard.
- Lavender or helichrysum essential oil.
- Antibiotic ointment.

Homeopathics:
- Cantharis 30c, alternatives: Causticum 30c, Urtica urens 30c.
- Arsenicum 30c or 200c for charred skin or burns with anxiety.
- Aconite 30c or Arnica 30c for shock and pain.
- Belladonna 30c for sunburn with fever and redness.
- Nat mur 30c for sunburn with dehydration and headache in a stoic person.

Herbal washes:
- Calendula, plantain, witch hazel, St. John's wort, nettle leaf.

COLDS & FLU

Twice a year for five years, in July and in October, I flew from Atlanta, Georgia to Colorado Springs, Colorado. In July, I arrived healthy and stayed healthy. In October, I developed sniffles on the plane that progressed to a cold.

After five years this no longer seemed to be a coincidence. Were there more germs in October? Were there more sneezing and wheezing people on the plane in October than in July? Why did I always catch cold in October but never in July? Why do so many people come down with the flu in the late fall and winter, but rarely in the summer?

Traditional Chinese Medicine (TCM) categorizes colds and flus as "external invasions of wind cold or wind heat." This suggests that colds and flus are more likely during windy weather, especially if we get chilled or overheated. When I traveled to Colorado Springs in October, I realized, I experienced a 20–30 degree temperature drop, and there was more wind in Colorado. This partially explained my October cold. But why didn't I catch cold in July? It was windy then, too. Why was I less immune to illness in the fall?

Thinking about the time of year provided a clue. Many researchers believe daily exposure to strong sunshine supports immune function. In July, we receive more sunshine than we do in October. In the fall and winter we wear more clothes, we have less exposure to sunlight because the days are shorter, we are more likely to stay indoors, and our immune function drops. Some researchers associate the rise and fall in immune function, and the numbers of colds and flus, with Vitamin D levels.

Although we ingest limited amounts of Vitamin D in a few foods, we primarily obtain it through sun exposure and supplementation. Without sun exposure or supplementation, our Vitamin D levels plummet. We become more vulnerable to colds and flu.

COLDS & FLU

Prevention Tactics

Get at least *20 minutes of sunshine daily*. When you are standing outside in the sun, so long as you are taller than your shadow, your body is manufacturing Vitamin D. During the winter, you will need to do this close to the noon hour. Clothing, sunscreen, and glass all block the sun so plan to be outside and at least partially uncovered during your sunbathing time. Sunshine is the ideal way to get your Vitamin D — you make it yourself! — and it's free. By the way, your body cannot overdose on Vitamin D manufactured from the sun. **Caution: Pay attention to strong sunshine — you still can get sunburned.** Also, if you have skin cancer, rely on Vitamin D_3 supplementation instead of sunshine.

Especially when we travel, we need *exercise* for its immunity-boosting effects. Take a walk! Go for a swim! Go to the gym! Our bodies defend against viruses by running a fever and thereby raising core body temperature. We can use exercise to increase core body temperature and reduce our viral load. This works before we get sick! Taking a brisk walk may curtail the sniffles or a sore throat.

Wash your hands. Often. Your hands pick up viruses and bacteria. Cleaning them frequently, preferably with soap and warm water, greatly reduces your viral load. Don't have access to soap and water? Use your hand sanitizer! (See the hand sanitizer recipe on page 186.)

Encourage sick friends and colleagues to stay in bed. Assume that if a person has symptoms, he or she is contagious. This is not the time for them to be hiking and biking. (Or infecting their travel companions.)

Throw away used tissues. Don't reuse. Viruses live, even on your used tissues. Don't save them.

Supplements

*Take **Vitamin D₃.*** If you tend to get colds or flu then take the Vitamin D challenge! Take 5,000 i.u. of Vitamin D₃ daily (3 times per day when you feel you are catching cold or flu or if you are ill), and do this for one year. Keep track of all your sick days in your calendar. At the end of the year, test your Vitamin D levels through your doctor or through an independent lab — you may wish to increase, decrease, or maintain your current dose. Vitamin D toxicity from too much Vitamin D supplementation is rare but possible: Dr. Andrew Weil states that no adverse effects have been reported with daily intakes of up to 10,000 i.u.

You are not doing the Vitamin D challenge? Take Vitamin D₃ in the doses above whenever you feel yourself becoming ill. This is an amazing remedy! If I could take only 1 remedy for the flu, this would be it! By the way, Vitamin D deficiency also is associated with cancer, fractures, autism, insulin resistance, diabetes, cardiovascular disease, and other ailments associated with modern (indoor) life. Vitamin D₃ is available in health food stores and online.

Take Vitamin C. Studies show that Vitamin C boosts immune function and is anti-viral. Take 1 gram daily for immune support and 3 grams daily if you are fighting a cold or flu. Some people take more — you will know that you have reached your limit if your stool becomes soft. Much higher levels have been used successfully for severe illnesses. Vitamin C is widely available.

Take zinc. Many people swear by this remedy, saying that they abort a cold if they take it immediately. Take 1 lozenge (20–25 mg) at the start of a cold or flu and repeat every 3 or 4 hours. Stop if you experience a metallic taste — that will tell you that you have had enough!

Food

Stop eating sugar. Eating sugar reduces immune function for hours. If the people around you are wheezing and sneezing, step away from the candy!

Stop eating phlegm-producing foods. Phlegm producing foods include dairy (especially non-raw and non-cultured dairy), sugar and sweets, grain-based products (especially wheat), and bananas. These foods make cold and flu symptoms worse.

Eat chicken soup. Yes, chicken soup really helps to both prevent and treat colds and flu.

Eat lemons. Lemons (and limes, to a lesser degree) help cut mucus and reduce congestion. Add the juice liberally to your water. To treat a cold and reduce congestion: cut a whole unpeeled organically grown lemon in quarters, blend with 8–12 ounces of water and a teaspoon of molasses, and drink daily.

Drink water. If you have nasal congestion, drinking plenty of water will help to thin your mucus and you will feel better.

Avoid cold foods, including ice. Hot soups and broths are especially good.

Rest

Get sufficient sleep. Keep your immune system strong by getting enough rest — most people need 8–9 hours every night for basic wellness. Really! When you become ill, take the time to "power sleep" — stay in bed and sleep or rest for at least 10–12 hours and schedule 3–4 hours to nap later that day. Sure, you can "tough it out" and continue working through a 7–10 day cold, but wouldn't it be so much better if you kicked it in 1–2 days instead?

73

COLDS & FLU

COLDS & FLU

Herbs

Reishi mushroom. Once I did a 1 year trial of reishi mushroom tincture, taking 1 dropperful before bed to assist with sleep. It helped with my sleep almost immediately. Nine months later, I noticed that I had been unusually healthy and had experienced no colds, no flu, and no allergy symptoms. I enjoy generally good health, but I do get sniffles especially when the weather turns cold. What a find! For cold and flu prevention, take 1 dropperful of reishi tincture, daily. It is available at health food stores and online.

Yin Chiao herbal formula. Yin Chiao is a Chinese herbal formula that includes honeysuckle and forsythia. Many of my clients take it at the first sign of cold or flu and do not get sick. Take 1 dropperful or 1 capsule hourly during waking hours while you feel a cold or flu coming on or for treatment if you get sick. I carry this with me on all trips.

Echinacea root. Echinacea has a well-deserved reputation for helping to stop a cold in its tracks. Take 1 teaspoon of the tincture when you first feel a cold or flu coming on; then take 1–4 dropperful of the tincture or 1–4 capsules hourly if you develop symptoms. This herb should be in everyone's travel kit.

Ginger. I love ginger. It is widely available around the world. Use it in any form: whole and raw from the grocery, pickled from an oriental market or restaurant, powdered, or in capsules or tincture. Take it whenever you become chilled, especially during cold and flu season. It will warm you, it helps fight viral infections, and additionally it helps relieve cold and flu symptoms. Take ginger hourly during waking hours for relief of symptoms.

Garlic is widely available throughout the world. I find that raw garlic is much more effective than cooked, but that both raw and cooked are more effective than dried, the form that's in tablets and capsules. Garlic is strongly antiviral and antibacterial and will be effective against a wide variety of pathogens. If you are getting sick or already have succumbed, plan to take a raw clove hourly. If you are quite brave, chew it up and swallow! It will burn all the way down but is very effective! Alternatively, mince, mix with honey, and wait 10 minutes before chewing and swallowing. Three or 4 whole cloves of garlic will help!

Oregano, thyme, and **rosemary** are culinary herbs that are antiviral and antibacterial. They are widely available in restaurants, food markets, and natural food stores. Make a strong tea by infusing 1 tablespoon of the dried leaves of any or all of these herbs in 1–2 cups of water and drink a cup 3–6 times daily. The taste is surprisingly strong! You can also use tinctures of these herbs if you have them — take 1 dropperful 3–6 times per day.

Homeopathic Remedies

The remedies listed below are recommended specifically for colds and flu, but may be very effective for other ailments, especially if the indications match. As a general rule, dissolve 1 pellet beneath your tongue and repeat every 30 minutes for a total of 3 doses. If you do not feel a change in your symptoms or if the remedy stops working for you, move on to another remedy. After your initial doses, take 1 pellet 3 times daily or as needed.

Oscillococcinum. This 200c potency homeopathic remedy is world renowned for both prevention and treatment of flu. I always bring it with me, just in case. A dose is a single pellet — NOT the entire tube! Each tube contains approximately 1,000 pellets. Your purchase will last you (and your friends and family) a lifetime. Dissolve 1 pellet beneath your tongue as soon as you feel even slightly "fluish." Repeat every 3 hours during waking hours or as needed for symptoms. Some travelers bring a tube with them as their only flu remedy. I use it only if no other homeopathic remedies are indicated.

Aconite 30c is the remedy to take for any illness that begins rapidly after exposure to cold, especially after exposure to cold wind. This is what I take if I have been hiking, become chilled, and feel a chill in my spine. Often, it will stop the cold or flu completely, but only if taken immediately.

Ferrum phosphoricum 30c is the most commonly prescribed homeopathic remedy in France. Taken at the very beginning of a cold, sore throat, or flu, this remedy may prevent the illness. It also can be used to treat an illness, particularly if there is inflammation, and may be used to reduce fever, especially in the 6x potency.

Eupatorium perfoliatum 30c is the homeopathic form of Boneset, an herb renowned for the treatment of flu. This remedy is specific for flu with deep bone pains.

Bryonia alba 30c is specific for flu with pain, especially when the pain is better with rest and worse with any motion. This flu usually begins slowly. If breathing is painful and you have flu symptoms, this is the remedy to choose first. Often, you will feel thirsty and irritable.

Gelsemium 30c is specific for flu with extreme fatigue. While anyone with the flu will feel tired, if you need Gelsemium you will feel that any movement is too much of an effort. (It even is tiring to hold open your eyes, and you may notice your eyes are half closed.) Often there is no thirst and you feel chilly.

Baptisia tinctoria 30c is specific for flu that begins rapidly with high fever. You may feel sore and bruised. Typically, your sweat, stool, and breath will smell bad, and you may have diarrhea.

Belladonna 30c is specific for flu that begins rapidly with high fever. This is the remedy to take if you feel hot, have a red face, and have a headache or other pains that throb. You may feel fearful and be delirious.

Arsenicum album 30c. Think of this remedy if you feel chilly and thirsty with clear nasal secretions, if you feel anxious and restless, and if you are nauseated with vomiting and diarrhea.

Nux vomica 30c. Try this remedy if you are very cold, irritable, nauseous, and overly concerned about getting back to work.

Rhus toxicodendrun 30c. Choose this remedy if you feel pain that is better with movement and is worse when you are sitting or lying still. You may find yourself moving to ease the pain, and you may feel chilly and thirsty. Often you have a dry sore throat.

Essential Oils

Several of my clients and friends rely on essential oils to protect them from viruses when they fly and are subject to recycled air. Fill a zipper-top plastic bag with 4–5 cotton balls moistened with a few drops of water. Add a total of 6–8 drops of any one or a combination of these essential oils: Tea tree, lavender, eucalyptus, rosemary, sage, oregano, thyme. (**Caution:** Rosemary is stimulating and can keep you awake.) Seal the bag and bring it with you. Open and breathe in the oils! Reseal when not in use. It will keep for several days. Using essential oils is NOT recommended if you are relying on homeopathic remedies or if you are receiving homeopathic constitutional treatment.

Colds & Flu Summary

Sunshine:

- Daily, when you are taller than the length of your shadow.

Exercise:

- Raise core body temperature to reduce viral load.
- Brisk walking.

Supplements:

- Vitamin D.
- Vitamin C.
- Zinc lozenges.

Food:

- Stop sugar and sweets.
- Stop phlegm-producing foods: dairy, grain-based products, and bananas.
- Eat chicken soup.
- Eat lemons.
- Drink water.

Rest:

- 8–9 hours nightly for wellness.
- Power sleep 10–12 hours at night, 3–4 hours during the day for when you are ill.

Prevention tactics:

- Wash your hands with soap and water.
- Encourage sick friends and colleagues to stay home.

Colds & Flu Summary, continued

Herbs:

- Reishi mushroom.
- Yin Chiao.
- Echinacea root.
- Ginger.
- Garlic.
- Oregano, thyme, rosemary.

Homeopathic remedies:

- Oscillococcinum.
- Aconite 30c.
- Ferrum phosphoricum 30c, 6x.
- Eupatorium perfoliatum 30c.
- Bryonia alba 30c.
- Baptisia tinctoria 30c.
- Belladonna 30c.
- Arsenicum album 30c.
- Nux vomica 30c.
- Rhus toxicodendrun 30c.

CONSTIPATION

Many of us get constipated when we travel. Why? Nerves, inactivity, lack of fluids, change of routine: these are all reasons. (Knowing why does not make us feel better!)

I once attended a meditation retreat where people were surreptitiously speaking in hushed tones and looking guilty. One was saying she always becomes constipated on these retreats, and the others were nodding. Several said that they had resigned themselves to suffering for the length of the retreat. I remembered that I also had this experience the last few times I had come there.

This had my attention. I studied the food, which was served buffet style. This is a great place, and the food is excellent. Was there too much starch, fat, salt, or sugar? No, the food is well planned and prepared. I found a wonderful combination of fresh salads, homemade breads, vegetables, and fish, poultry, or meat at every meal. There was plenty of fiber. The problem wasn't the food (although some people will lock up whenever their diet changes, regardless of food quality).

Knowing that travel can dry us, I increased my consumption of water. Every waking hour, I drank at least 8–10 ounces of water. (That resulted in more than a gallon of water a day! You have to know I was determined.) Well, soon I was very well hydrated and visiting the bathroom every hour. I also was able to move my bowels. Drinking more water really helped! Others noticed what I was doing and found similar results. Still, I had to strain.

Every day, we had a movement class. One day, we were making drumming noises, rhythmically patting our lower abdomens. After doing this for 5 or 10 minutes, I began feeling movement in my bowels. That day, there was no strain. Of course! Here we were, like at most conferences, spending our time sitting. In a way, stagnating. Add movement, and the stagnation clears. Interestingly, long walks were not enough (although they often do the trick). Our bodies required more direct stimulation.

Herbal Recommendations for Constipation

If you are planning a trip and you commonly become constipated, pack a remedy for it. My favorite herbal remedy for travel is *Smooth Move tea*. Widely available in many supermarkets, health food stores, and online, purchase the tea bags by the box. Formulated by herbalist Rosemary Gladstar, it addresses constipation resulting from different causes. It works very well and does not result in diarrhea. Steep one teabag in hot water for at least 5 minutes, and drink. It works even better if you can steep it for 10 or more minutes. Drink 1 cup of tea 1–3 times per day. (By the way, Gladstar receives no compensation for Smooth Move sales - if you love the tea, buy it and also buy her books!)

If I couldn't find Smooth Move tea, I would use *cascara sagrada*, a herbal bowel tonic. It works best in tincture form. The standard dose is 1–3 droppersful, taken before bed. If you have taken that dose and do not move your bowels the following day, I recommend increasing the number of doses to 2 per day and, if necessary, to 3 per day. Substitutes for cascara sagrada include *rhubarb* and *senna*; both are available in tincture form. Take them at the same dose and frequency as cascara sagrada.

Ground *psyllium seed* is the herb of choice for many people. It is a pure bulking agent that is the primary ingredient of Metamucil, the popular over-the-counter preparation for constipation. For many people, psyllium helps compensate for the reduced fiber in travel

81

food. People find that it softens their stool and makes it easier to expel. **Caution: You MUST drink sufficient water or psyllium can cause bloating!** This is NOT the herb for you if you refuse to drink water. To take, stir one rounded teaspoonful into 8 ounces of water and drink immediately. (If you stir and wait, the water will solidify.) Take 1–3 times per day. Many people add this to their protein drink or to their morning juice. I add a pinch of ground fennel or ginger to prevent bloating.

Triphala is a famous remedy from the Ayurvedic tradition (the Asian Indian medical system) that normalizes bowel function through its balancing effect on the three doshas (the three Ayurvedic metaphors that describe body function). Not surprisingly, it is the most widely used herbal formula in the world and is used by millions of people every day. It also is a bowel tonic that strengthens bowel function and may be taken safely for years. Take 2 capsules 1–3 times per day. Alternatively, stir one teaspoon of triphala powder into 8 ounces of hot water, wait until the powder settles to the bottom, and drink the water. Feel free to reuse the powder a second time that day. The dose of the powder is 1 teaspoon taken 2 times per day.

Homeopathic Recommendations

If you possess a "shy" colon — you might move your bowels if only everyone would leave you alone for an hour — try homeopathic *Natrum mur* 30c. The number of doses varies: dissolve 1 pellet beneath your tongue 1–3 times per day. You also can use this remedy for cold sores!

If your constipation results from over-indulging in food or drink, try homeopathic *Nux vomica* 30c. Dissolve 1 pellet beneath your tongue 1–3 times per day. You also can use this remedy for hangovers!

If your constipation is from dehydration, try homeopathic *Bryonia* 30c. Dissolve 1 pellet beneath your tongue 1–3 times per day. Try it for dry, hacking coughs. See "Choosing Homeopathic Remedies," page 21.

If your constipation does not fit any of the descriptions above, try homeopathic *Alumina* 30c. Dissolve 1 pellet beneath your tongue 1 time per day.

Food Recommendations

The best food remedy for constipation is *prune juice or stewed prunes*. For many people, 6 ounces (juice glass) or 8 ounces (water glass) of prune juice, once a day, is sufficient. Find the juice in supermarkets and in pharmacies (in the food section). Many hotels and restaurants offer stewed prunes at breakfast: try to eat at least 8–10 prunes. Alternatively, try *figs*. In season, you can find them fresh—they are scrumptious! Many grocery stores stock both dried prunes and dried figs; eating 8–12 of either will keep most people moving. Most groceries carry prune juice in quart bottles or in 6 packs of 6 ounce cans. The quart bottles provide a better value if you have access to refrigeration.

Generally, to relieve constipation, *increase fiber and decrease refined starches*. For some people, the choice of a bran muffin in place of a bagel, biscuit, or piece of toast will be sufficient, and many hotels, cruise ships, and restaurants have them. Some people like to carry *flax seeds* to top their salads and increase fiber—use at least 2 tablespoons per day. Some people find that eating a whole grapefruit in the morning guarantees a bowel movement the next morning, but grapefruit juice usually does not have the same effect. **Caution: Cooked fruits and vegetables are safer travel choices than raw, especially in areas where water quality or restaurant cleanliness is poor.** See the "Parasites" section for more information.

Avoiding certain foods greatly aids in elimination. Highly refined foods, such as *bread, cake,* and *cookies* literally gum up the works. In elementary school we made an incredible, immovable glue by mixing white flour with water and a pinch of salt. I've often wondered about how we metabolize this very same combination when we eat flour-based products. From my experience and that of many travelers, eating fewer breads, cakes, and cookies helps to keep things moving. Additionally avoiding white rice, pasta, instant mashed potatoes, instant oatmeal, and instant "any starch" also will help. Personally, I reserve white rice for times when I have loose stool — it stops it fast!

Eating *eggs* can result in constipation, especially if you are eating more of them than usual. This does not mean that eggs are bad for you, just that you need to compensate for the arachidonic acid in them. If eggs are constipating you, take 1–2 capsules of fish oil or essential fatty acids daily. Your constipation likely will clear.

Coffee stimulates bowel function. If you always drink coffee while at home but NOT when you travel and you become constipated when you travel, the lack of coffee may be the source of your constipation! You may need to compensate — try one of the herbal remedies listed at the top of this section.

Private Time

Give yourself *private time* for elimination. Many people have a "shy" colon; they will not eliminate on demand and certainly not in the presence of others. Others simply need sufficient time, which often seems unavailable while traveling. If this is you, find the time and the place where you have what you need. For some, this means going down to the hotel lobby early in the morning for a private "walk." No one needs to know how you spend most of your walk time.

Exercise

Take a walk! Run. Bike. Work out. When we travel, we often fail to exercise. The lack of movement leads to a lack of colon activity. The cure may be as simple as getting up and walking for 20 minutes. There's no place to walk? When indoors, take the stairs and walk the halls. Outdoors, walk around the site where you are staying. In your room, do yoga, tai chi, qi gong. Many hotels and cruise ships have exercise rooms at no additional charge. Use them. Many cruise ships additionally have an outside path circling the ship on one deck, designated for walking.

Self Massage

Circular tummy rubs, following the direction of the colon, may assist with elimination. Your colon begins near the crease between your right hip and thigh, travels up towards your ribs, goes horizontally from the right to the left and travels down along your left side, towards the center and then out. Using the palm of one or both hands, make clockwise circles on your abdomen, following the course of colon. Doing this for 5 or more minutes per day adds energy to your system, may counter the stagnation of prolonged sitting, is pleasant, and costs nothing.

Herbal Remedies in the Wilderness

Prepare your own psyllium seed substitute from the seeds of the *plantain* plant! (*Plantago psyllium*, a kind of plantain, is the only source of psyllium seeds, but the seeds of other plantain species will work almost as well.) Soak 1 or more teaspoons of the seeds in a cup of water overnight and drink or add to cooking liquids the next day. Alternatively, chew and swallow 1 teaspoon of the seeds or simmer as a tea. Take 1–3 times per day. I have chewed fresh plantain seed on treks in North America, Europe, Asia, Africa, and Australia. It is easy to spot, and it always helps.

The roots of the *dandelion*, *yellow dock* (also *curly dock*), or *Solomon's seal* plants, found widely throughout North America and on other continents, serve as laxatives. Simmer 1 tablespoon of the cleaned and minced root in 2 cups of water for 20–30 minutes, cool, and drink 2–3 times per day.

CONSTIPATION

Constipation Summary

To avoid or eliminate constipation:

- Water: Drink 64–128 ounces per day.
- Exercise: Walking, running, yoga, tai chi, ANYTHING that keeps you moving.
- Herbs: Smooth Move teabags. Take cascara sagrada, psyllium seed, triphala. Other herbs include senna and rhubarb.
- Foods: Eat prunes, figs, or grapefruit. Avoid starch, salt, and sugar. Increase fiber. Combine foods properly.
- Find privacy and time for elimination.
- Perform circular tummy rubs.

Top choices of packable constipation remedies (you only need one):

- Cascara sagrada tincture.
- Triphala capsules.
- Homeopathic: Natrum mur. 30c, Nux vomica 30c, Bryonia 30c.

Top wilderness choices:

- Plantain seed.
- Dandelion root.
- Yellow dock root.
- Solomon's seal root.

DEHYDRATION

Late one night I received an emergency call from a friend's husband. He reported that my friend had been staggering, had been dizzy, had lost her balance, and had fallen. I knew that she did not take drugs and did not use alcohol. She had not hit her head but she had a terrible headache and was nauseated. Could I come quickly?

My friend was in bed and did not speak or look at me. Her face was pale and her skin felt cold. I asked what had happened. Her husband explained that she had eaten bad food and suffered with days of vomiting and diarrhea. She had been so sick that she had soaked her bed clothes with sweat. He reported that she had recovered from the bad food but that these new symptoms started the next day. My friend asked if I thought she was dying.

My friend was dehydrated! Yes, she was in an extreme state and required immediate hydration. I asked that she agree to drink 1/2 cup of water with electrolytes every 15 minutes for the next 4 hours, and that she drink 1 cup per waking hour for the next 2 days. I also requested that her husband bring her to the bathroom whenever she needed to go. I requested that she have no coffee or tea for the next week. If they could not comply with my requests, I would call 911!

My friend and her husband agreed. I gave her a single pellet of homeopathic Arsenicum 200c. She immediately sighed. I prepared an electrolyte mix with powdered ginger. Her husband mixed it into water and she began sipping moments later. Her nausea ended within moments and her headache was gone within the hour. Two hours later she was sitting up in bed and talking. Success!

About Dehydration

Dehydration occurs when we lose more fluids than we take in, usually through urination, diarrhea, sweating, or vomiting. Expect dehydration when engaging in prolonged walking or other athletics, from long exposure to the sun or high temperature, from low humidity (desert or arid areas, airline flights, air conditioning and heating) and high altitude. Also expect dehydration from taking diuretics — substances that increase urination — such as coffee, tea, alcohol, many blood pressure medications, and some other medications. Even mild dehydration damages athletic performance; moderate dehydration can result in anxiety, fatigue, headaches, loss of balance, dizziness, and feeling faint. Severe dehydration can result in death. If your urine is darkening or you need to urinate less frequently, you are becoming dehydrated.

Treating Dehydration

Drink pure water! Water. Not coffee. Not tea. Not beer, wine, or spirits—water. Beer, wine, and other alcoholic beverages are diuretics, which cause you to urinate more of your fluids away.

Dehydration results in a loss of minerals, changing the balance of electrolytes in your bloodstream and reducing your ability to hold onto fluids. Adding minerals to your water restores electrolyte balance and increases water retention, which you need when you are becoming dehydrated. Replenish your electrolytes by adding electrolytes to your water. Ever drink Gatorade (G series or a sports recovery drink)? Adding 8–16 ounces of *Gatorade* to 16 ounces of water and drinking the mixture instead of plain water will help maintain your electrolyte balance. (Straight Gatorade is too sugary and salty to use in place of water). Want to pack it with you? Packets of *EmergenC* or *ElectroMix* powder, added to 12–16 ounces of water, provide an excellent electrolyte mixture. I always pack EmergenC or ElectroMix, just in case.

On the road? Add 1/4 teaspoon of salt plus 2-1/2 teaspoons of sugar to 16 ounces of water. Estimated amounts are fine! From a coffee shop, gas station, or fast food restaurant, add 1 individual sized packet of salt and 3 packets of sugar (NOT artificial sweeteners) to a 16–24 ounce bottle of water. If you have it, additionally add 1/4 teaspoon of baking soda, 1/8 teaspoon of salt substitute (potassium salt), and a tablespoon of lemon juice (or a squeeze of lemon). Can't do the sugar? Substitute real maple syrup, honey, or agave, or substitute ½ cup of fruit juice for the sugar. This is amazingly helpful! It will keep you hydrated, and will help to eliminate the symptoms of dehydration.

What about foods, homeopathic remedies, herbs, and supplements? Dehydration is caused by not having enough water. Drink water.

If you drink a lot of water but still are chronically dehydrated, you may have a condition that Traditional Chinese Medicine (TCM) calls yin deficiency. It is fairly common and the incidence increases with age. One TCM formula for this is called *Rehmannia Six* or *Liu Wei Di Huang*. It is available from Chinese herb shops, some natural food markets, and online. Consider seeing a practitioner.

Dehydration Summary

- Drink water.
- Drink water with electrolytes.
- Avoid coffee, tea, alcohol, and other diuretics.

DIARRHEA

On a camping trip to Cumberland Island off the coast of Georgia I encountered a family with a 7-year-old with a tummy ache who was having diarrhea every 10 minutes. We knew why; he had eaten much of his Mom's diet cookie stash in about an hour. Cumberland Island is remote, has no medical facilities, and is connected to the mainland by a ferry that comes 2 times a day, 5–7 days per week. What could we do?

We had to re-hydrate the child and slow the diarrhea. To a quart (32 ounces) bottle of water, we added 6 packs of sugar and a small packet (about ⅛ teaspoon) of salt. We shook the bottle and gave the unhappy but cooperative patient 4 ounces every 15 minutes. That covered the re-hydration. To slow the diarrhea we thought to use the BRAT diet. We needed banana (we had none), rice (ditto), apple (ditto), or toasted bread (also none). But they had a package of rice cakes! Rice cakes would be perfect, especially burnt. We skewered the rice cake with a twig and "toasted" it until black over their one-burner camping stove. After adding some grape jelly (his request!), he chewed and swallowed ¼ of that dry and blackened rice cake. We told him how proud we were of him and joked about his blackened tongue and teeth. Ninety minutes after eating the burnt rice cake, his tummy ache was gone. He moved his bowels only 1 additional time that day after eating the burnt rice cake. Success!

Diarrhea can spoil any trip. People experiencing it — most of us have — can be totally miserable! In a youngster, it can be especially debilitating. Diarrhea is very dehydrating and requires continual drinking of large quantities of water to avoid the extreme fatigue that often accompanies it. It can prevent the sufferer and her companions from any travel beyond the nearest bathroom or rest station. Left to run its course, diarrhea easily can continue for 48–72 hours.

Dealing with Diarrhea

Luckily, anywhere in the world, you can find great remedies for diarrhea that work. You can purchase herbal or pharmaceutical remedies for your travel kit, you can find food remedies in restaurants and food stores, and you can even find remedies in the woods.

Water and Diarrhea

Regardless of how you choose to treat your diarrhea, *drink water*. Drink a lot of water. Drink more than you feel comfortable drinking. Why? Diarrhea is one of the most dehydrating conditions you can experience. The dehydration is responsible for much of the fatigue and will lengthen your recovery. Diarrhea can be life-threatening, especially for a child or an elderly person. Yes, you can die from diarrhea. So drink! Drink at least 4 ounces every 15 minutes or 8 ounces every 30 minutes when experiencing frequent or severe diarrhea.

Add electrolytes to your water. (See "Dehydration.")

Food and Diarrhea

What can you safely eat if you suddenly have diarrhea? Certain foods work extremely well. Remember the *BRAT diet* recommended for children? Consisting of bananas, (white) rice, apples (grated and allowed to brown), and toast (burnt), this diet includes two excellent remedies. *Burnt toast*, available around the world, is a form of charcoal, and will both detoxify your system and eventually stop diarrhea. (See the section below on charcoal.) Burn toast until it blackens, crumble, and then crush, stir a teaspoon into 4 ounces of water or *black tea* and drink. Tea contains tannic acid, which also helps stop diarrhea. *White rice* will solidify your stool. So will *whey protein*, which is widely available.

While you are suffering from diarrhea, avoid laxative foods. Sugar alcohols such as sorbitol and mannitol, used to sweeten many diet foods (the Mom's diet cookies!) with fewer calories or carbs, cause diarrhea when people eat too much of them. (Even 2 or 3 diet cookies may be too much.) Foods recommended for treating constipation, such as prunes and figs, will increase diarrhea. *Eliminate coffee* — it stimulates bowel activity. If you are gluten sensitive, unaccustomed gluten or cross-contamination of your food with gluten may cause diarrhea. If you are sensitive to sugar or sweets, cut back. Too much sugar can cause diarrhea.

If your diarrhea is yellow or green and extremely smelly, try eating *watermelon* — at least 1 cup 3 times per day or ½ cup every hour. I used this remedy one time in response to frequent (10 times in 3 hours!), explosive, smelly, and hot diarrhea, and after 1 cup of watermelon the diarrhea stopped! Afterwards, I could not eat any other foods — they all made my stomach turn — but watermelon was fine. Chinese herbal medicine considers watermelon a refrigerant (a food that will cool you down). It really is! Reserve watermelon for summertime and for when you have hot stool.

Umeboshi plum is a wonderful oriental remedy for diarrhea. Studies show that constituents of umeboshi are anti-bacterial. Umeboshi works particularly well at eliminating dysentery and the staphylococci bacteria. Purchase prepared umeboshi (paste or whole plums) in oriental stores or in natural food stores in the macrobiotic section. Although umeboshi usually is used as a very salty and sour condiment, you can use it as a medicinal food. Take approximately 1 teaspoon — or 1 plum — every 2 hours until the diarrhea clears. You also can take umeboshi mashed into rice or simmered in tea.

DIARRHEA

Mung beans and mung bean tea are another remedy for diarrhea. Mung beans are detoxifying and treat food poisoning, dysentery, pesticide poisoning, boils, hot skin rashes, and heat exhaustion. They are especially useful at clearing diarrhea accompanied by fever or sweating. Small and olive-green, mung beans are the un-sprouted version of bean sprouts. Purchase them dried in Oriental food stores or in natural food stores. To cook, simmer one cup of mung beans in 4 cups of water for 1½ hours (you may begin sipping the simmered water after only 20 minutes). Both the cooked beans and the water clear diarrhea. Although this may sound like too mild a remedy, I know of cases where mung bean tea did the trick when nothing else worked. Drink half a cup to one cup per hour. When you feel strong enough for solid food, eat the beans.

Drugstore Remedy

Most pharmacists recommend a product called *Imodium* that is available without a prescription. It is effective for diarrhea resulting from a wide variety of causes, including spoiled food, bacteria, viruses, and even parasites. Follow directions on the label. Often, one pill is sufficient to stop diarrhea. It is reliable, and many seasoned travelers carry it with them.

Natural Food Store Remedies

I recommend that travelers carry *grapefruit seed extract* (GSE) with them. For travelers with a tendency towards diarrhea, or if you are traveling back country or in an area known for causing digestive upset, take 1 dropperful, 5–10 drops, or 1 capsule daily. If you feel gurgling in your bowels or you begin to have diarrhea, take the above dose 3 times per day, increasing the frequency to hourly if diarrhea develops. When I have taken this remedy daily, I have NOT developed diarrhea, even in some very challenging environments.

If diarrhea follows exposure to cold (you go swimming on a cold day and you don't cover up after coming out of the water), try *ginger* from your kit. (See "Making a Travel Kit.") Chances are the ginger will sufficiently heat your chilled system and the diarrhea will end. Quickly.

Homeopathic Remedies

In some areas, homeopathic remedies are the easiest medicines to find, and the little plastic vials that hold tiny pellets are convenient to carry. I generally recommend the potency of 30c. See "Choosing Homeopathic Remedies," page 21. *Nux vomica* 30c works for the overworked, irritable, and chilly traveler who has been eating too much and too many heavy foods. You may be the person who feels the frequent urge to defecate but often cannot. It is good for the workaholic with alternating diarrhea and constipation. Did you overeat? Did you drink too much? Take 1 pellet every 15 minutes until symptoms cease, and again if symptoms return.

Arsenicum 30c works for the exhausted and restless traveler with explosive diarrhea and vomiting. It's also a good choice for food poisoning or when you feel pain at your stomach. Try it whenever you have both diarrhea and vomiting — 1 pellet every 15 minutes until symptoms cease and again if symptoms return. If Arsenicum fails, and if you feel cold and have both diarrhea and vomiting, take *Veratrum album* 30c, 1 pellet every 15 minutes until symptoms cease and again if symptoms return. Consider *Podophyllum* 30c for yellow diarrhea, especially if it is frequent and painless and if there also is nausea or vomiting. Take 1 pellet every 15 minutes until symptoms cease and again if symptoms return. *Gelsemium* 30c helps the nervous traveler who knows her diarrhea results from anxiety — it's the performer's remedy. *Pulsatilla* 30c helps those who have over-indulged in rich foods who have diarrhea at night. *Sulphur* 30c helps travelers with "cock's crow" diarrhea, the kind that occurs painlessly at dawn. The dosage for all these homeopathic remedies for diarrhea is the same: take 1 pellet every 15 minutes until the symptoms cease and again if symptoms return.

Charcoal

Charcoal is a VERY GOOD remedy for all sorts of food and chemical poisoning. It is used by a wide range of healthcare providers, including medical doctors, herbalists, and naturopathic physicians. Unlike Imodium, charcoal not only stops the diarrhea but also helps to eliminate the toxicity that may be the cause. Think of charcoal as acting much like a sponge that attracts and holds many times its own weight in toxins. The toxins bind to the charcoal and are then eliminated through the colon.

Activated charcoal is the most compact form, and I recommend that you carry it with you. You can find activated charcoal in pills and capsules and in powdered form in pharmacies and health food stores. Charcoal capsules work well for many people and are easily packed. The dose is 2 capsules every hour until diarrhea stops, then 2 capsules 1–3 times per day. In extreme cases, you can take more. To use the powdered form, stir 1–3 teaspoons of charcoal in 1 cup of water and swallow.

Need it NOW? Make your own vegetable charcoal by burning bread, popcorn, or any starchy food to a crisp. To be most effective, the charred food should be deep black and snap when you break it. Vegetable charcoal works very well, but you will need to use more of it than you would the activated charcoal. Use 1–2 tablespoons of vegetable charcoal for each dose. To make it easier to take, crush it and dissolve in water.

Charcoal will temporarily turn your teeth, gums, and tongue black! Just continue rinsing with water. It also will turn your stool black — so don't panic. And when charcoal first goes through your system, it provides additional force to your bowel movement.

Clay

Bentonite clay, available in health food stores, will slow and later stop diarrhea while helping detoxify the colon. The dose is 1 tablespoon dissolved in water. This remedy is often taken long term to help clear toxicity in the body, but it also works well short term. If you choose to gather your own clay, you must heat it for at least one hour in a 225–250 degree oven to kill the likely bacteria in the clay. No, I don't know how to find edible clay in the wild! You are on your own if you choose to gather clay. Better yet, if you are in an area known for this use of clay, seek out an expert.

Diarrhea in the Wilderness

What if you are in the wild? The root (preferably) or leaf from any *blackberry* or *raspberry* vine is VERY effective. I recommend making a tea by cleaning and simmering a quarter cup to half cup of the cut-up root or leaf in 2 cups of water for at least 10–30 minutes. While you are waiting, chewing a piece of the cleaned root will help. *Grape vine* also will help. Make a tea of a 1 or 2 large handsful (2 ounces) of the fresh leaf simmered in a quart of water for at least 10–30 minutes. *Wild strawberry root and leaf* and *blueberry leaf* also work but are slightly less effective. Prepare them same way that you would prepare the blackberry or raspberry tea. Drink a cup of tea per hour until the diarrhea clears.

You are in the woods? Do you see any weeping willow trees? Easily identified, the bark of the *willow tree* is high in tannic acid, a known astringent. Willow

97

DIARRHEA

bark tea is a good remedy for diarrhea. The inner bark of the *white oak* (white oak is especially good, the bark of other oaks will work) also makes a tea that will stop diarrhea. Prune some small branches and cut the inner bark in strips. Simmer approximately 1 tablespoon of bark in one and a half cups of water for 20–30 minutes. Drink half a cup every 30 minutes.

You can make your own *charcoal* remedy by burning the wood from trees, shrubs, or other plant matter, so long as the part you are using is traditionally used for food or medicine. Some plant parts may be toxic, including tomato vines. **Don't use something that is toxic or something you can't identify.** Burning any edible starch and eating the resulting charcoal will work. Starch includes rice, potatoes, grits, bread, and corn products. You also can char and eat *kudzu root* if you are in the southeastern United States! **Caution: Do not ingest the kind of charcoal used for grilling or starting fires.**

Diarrhea Summary

To avoid or eliminate diarrhea:

Water:	Drink plenty of pure water.
Foods:	B.R.A.T. diet. (bananas, white rice, (brown) grated apple, burned toast). Avoid laxative foods, such as sugar alcohols and some dried fruit. Strictly avoid gluten and soy if gluten sensitive. Whey protein. Umeboshi plum. Mung beans and mung bean tea.
Herbs:	Blackberry root or cranesbill (also known as geranium). Ginger (if diarrhea resulted from exposure to cold).
Homeopathics:	Nux vomica 30c. Arsenicum 30c. Gelsemium 30c. Pulsatilla 30c. Sulphur 30c.
Other:	Activated charcoal. Bentonite clay.
Drugs:	Imodium.

Top choices of packable remedies:

- Blackberry root tincture.
- Activated charcoal capsules.
- Nux vomica 30c.
- Imodium.

Top wilderness remedies:

- Wild blackberry, raspberry, or strawberry leaf and root.
- White oak tree inner bark.
- Willow tree bark.
- Charcoal (not the kind used for grilling or for starting fires!)

FOOD

Flying from Mongolia to Russia, I became terribly ill, with frequent vomiting and diarrhea. The flight lasted 7 hours, and I was sick for all of it. My seat-mate, an experienced world traveler, opined that I had drunk "bad water." I remembered dashing to the airport and eating a protein bar and drinking a half cup of coffee — lukewarm — on the way. Yes, the water could have been bad, likely contaminated with parasites. Parasites would give these symptoms.

I arrived in my Moscow hotel room, struggling with my repeated bathroom trips, my abdominal pain, and my fatigue. I felt so disappointed — here I was in one of the great cities of the world, and I didn't want to leave my room. I took natural and pharmaceutical remedies for the bad water but did not improve. Hungry and wanting to keep up my calories, I nibbled on a protein bar. The vomiting and diarrhea continued. I stayed in Moscow for 4 days, spending most of the time in my room, primarily eating the food in my backpack. When I finally returned home, the vomiting and diarrhea ended, but it took me months to fully recover.

A year later I attended a lecture about hidden food ingredients and learned that "modified food starch" could be manufactured from wheat. I thought of that protein bar I had eaten just prior to boarding the flight from Mongolia to Russia and then ate to "keep up my calories" throughout my Moscow stay. Could that have been the problem? As someone who is gluten intolerant, this is very important! I raced to a store, found the bar, looked at the list of ingredients, and found it. Modified food starch! Was it wheat? I phoned the company and asked the source of their modified food starch. The person I spoke with did not know, said there was no way to find out, and went on to say the company advised that anyone with a gluten sensitivity avoid their bars. Done! I will never eat their bars again!

I had made myself sick by eating a food to which I am wildly allergic. I made several mistakes I don't intend to repeat. I'll be more careful and scrutinize ingredient lists on packaged foods I buy. If a food manufacturer cannot or will not identify what is in a food, I will not eat it. Ever. If a food manufacturer lists an ingredient so that the ingredient is not identifiable, I will not eat it.

What Do I Eat?

I eat real food and a lot of it! I enjoy my food. I eat eggs, meat, poultry, fish, brightly colored vegetables, salads, baked squash, occasional organic fruit and berries in season, unsalted nuts and seeds, and very dark chocolate. I love having a cup of coffee or tea in the morning. I do not eat gluten, contained in wheat, spelt, rye, barley, most cous cous, and most oats. Ever. They make me sick, and I don't need that, especially when I'm away from home. I avoid all flour and grain products, even whole grain products, including corn and rice, because they make me fat and sleepy. I eat limited sugar as a rare treat; I rarely eat it because sugar makes me fat and reduces immune function. I refuse all artificial sweeteners, including aspartame (typically in blue packets), saccharin (typically in pink packets), and sucralose (typically in yellow packets), and all sugar alcohols.

I enjoy full-fat dairy products such as cream in my coffee, unsweetened yogurt, and (occasionally) ice cream. I eat organic and locally grown whenever possible. I avoid eating chemicals or genetically modified foods (GMOs).

My style of eating, called "paleo" or "primal," is naturally low in starch and sugar. Research increasingly supports this eating style for increasing energy levels and improving athletic performance, immune

101

FOOD

function, general health, memory, and alertness. It also decreases cholesterol and blood sugar. And oh, yes, it also promotes fat loss.

General Principles for Choosing What to Eat

As a general rule, *eat the highest quality food*, organic when possible, with minimal processing, little or no chemicals, without high fructose corn syrup, and without soy (to which so many people are sensitive). Check the labels and avoid MSG (monosodium glutamate), which adds flavor but creates headaches and illness for many people, and aspartame. I also recommend that you reduce or eliminate wheat.

Drink a glass of water before you choose what to eat. When traveling, most of us are in a chronic state of dehydration. Dehydration affects our food choices, making us feel hunger more acutely and causing us to desire more sugar and more starch. In short, we order and consume more food when we are dehydrated than when we are not. Get your water first, and drink up!

Keep drinking your water. Travel, except in high humidity areas, is dehydrating. Plane travel is especially dehydrating. Many of us drink less so that we won't have to find and use a bathroom in a strange place. Many of us drink more coffee, tea, and alcohol when we travel, and all three are diuretics that dehydrate us. Not only will dehydration affect our food choices, it also will cause us to feel more anxious and to have more trouble falling and staying asleep. And it leads to wrinkles.

Eat "real food" in its original form or close to it, prepared in a traditional manner. "Real food" looks like what it is – broccoli, peaches, and almonds are great examples. Traditional methods of food preparation include heating (grilling, roasting, steaming, boiling, stewing, and braising), drying, and fermenting.

Fresh or dehydrated blueberries are real food, but blueberry flavored powdered whey protein packets are not.

Real food spoils. If your food has a multiple year unrefrigerated shelf life, it likely is not real food. Choose food that spoils, but eat it before it does. (Sure, I make an exception for the food that I pack with me on trips. Make your travel food as "real" as you can!)

Real food that I recommend includes meat, poultry, fish, and eggs; fresh or recently cooked vegetables; whole fruit (including olives and avocados); and nuts and seeds. Some people thrive with the addition of dairy products such as cheese and yogurt. Many people add in beans – they are more difficult to digest but are important foods for vegetarians and can be convenient travel foods.

Eat enough protein, contained in meat, poultry, fish, eggs, dairy, and beans. Protein can be more expensive, less available, and less convenient than starch and sugar so people often eat less of it when they travel. Eating less protein than they need, people begin breaking down muscle fiber and then become fatigued — who needs that?

How much protein do we need? Experts agree that we need to eat substantial portions of protein daily. According to some nutritionists, a 150 pound person needs at least 55 grams, a 200 pound person needs at least 74 grams, and a 250 pound person needs at least 92 grams daily. Other nutritionists find these figures way too low! Some also consider lean body mass and level of activity in their calculations and arrive at substantially higher recommendations. To make things easy, think of 20–35 grams of protein being the minimum you need for each of 3 meals daily. For more specific information, consult the book *Protein Power* by Michael R. Eades, MD and Mary Dan Eades, MD.

What food portions provide the protein we require?

FOOD

Rounding, you obtain approximately 7 grams of protein from any of the following: 1 egg, 1 ounce of animal protein, 4 ounces of cooked beans, ¼ cup of nuts or seeds, or 2 tablespoons of nut butter. Three eggs contain approximately 21 grams of protein and provide sufficient protein for one meal, especially if supplemented with cheese or meat. Twelve ounces of cooked beans — a cup and a half — provides a similar amount of protein. A 4 ounce portion of cooked meat, poultry, or fish provides approximately 28 grams of protein.

Choose the highest quality protein you can afford. Eat wild caught fish, grassfed meat, and organic or pastured poultry and eggs. Not only do they taste better but they also are more nutritious. I have spoken to many people who resumed eating meat (following years of doing without) once they tasted grassfed meat. Think you can't afford wild caught fish? All sardines are wild caught, widely available, and packaged for travel!

Eat dairy if you can digest it. Dairy products include milk, cream, butter, yogurt, and cheese. Many people cannot digest dairy — I am not recommending dairy products if they give you any symptoms! If you eat them, choose organic, full-fat dairy products from grassfed cows. For people who can digest it, this is a very good food. See the book *Nourishing Traditions* by Sally Fallon and Mary Enig for more information.

Choose colorful carbohydrates. When it comes to carbohydrates, choose brightly colored vegetables and avoid white or brown ones. Generally speaking, brightly colored vegetables are more nutritious, easier to digest, and lower in starch and sugar. White and brown carbohydrates tend to be high in sugar or starch that converts rapidly to sugar. Typical white and brown carbohydrate foods include grains (wheat, corn, oats, and rice) white potatoes, and legumes (beans and peanuts), all of which are high in starch and/or sugar. As

104

a general rule, the more highly colored fruits and vegetables are more nutritious and better tolerated.

Limit sugar and starch. Most breads, crackers, cereal, cakes, cookies, pies, and candy are high in carbohydrates and specifically high in sugars and starch. Potato and corn chips similarly are high in starch and also may be very high in salt and damaged fats. If you eat too much sugar and starch, you will feel sick. You will feel tired. You may become bloated. You may find that your thinking is unclear. Our bodies metabolize all carbohydrates to sugar, and too much sugar drags us down. Check out *Good Calories, Bad Calories* by Gary Taubes and *Wheat Belly* by William Davis, MD for more information about the effects of these foods.

Avoid grain-based products. Much processed food consists largely of grain-based carbohydrates and sugar, which are inexpensive and don't require refrigeration. I recommend you avoid grain-based products as food and eat them only as fun snacks. Yes, that includes bread. In my experience, most people are sensitive to grain-based products (especially wheat), and most of them don't know it. Do you get tired after lunch? It could be the starch: 2 slices of bread for your sandwich, the tortilla for your burrito, the potato, or the rice that accompanies your Asian meal. Substitute vegetables (all colors except white and brown) for your starch, and you may find yourself less tired. Grain-based products also may give you reflux or a belly ache. Try doing without and see if those problems cease.

Avoid fried food, especially when traveling. Most commercially fried food contains trans fats that are potentially cancer causing. Due to the high frying temperatures, most frying oil has become damaged; this oil is inflaming to your body and may contribute to aging, cancer, arterial blockages, and weight gain. Many commercial frying oils have become rancid from repeat-

105

FOOD

ed use. They can give you a stomach ache, cause abdominal distress, and may lead to other problems.

Avoid trans fats. Hydrogenation, a chemical process that delays spoilage, reduces "greasiness," and solidifies oil (such as turning corn oil into margarine) is the source of most trans fats. Don't eat commercial baked products (most pre-packaged and unrefrigerated breads, cookies, cakes, and pies) especially if they contain partially hydrogenated oils or trans fats. Reports from leading medical institutions and health groups indicate that virtually all trans fats are unhealthy and contribute to heart disease. (The small amounts of trans fat that naturally occurs in some meats, milk, and cheese don't seem to be damaging.). Trans fats are highly inflammatory and literally make us sick!

Avoid chemicals and additives. If you need to carry shelf-stable foods with you when you travel, read labels and compare products to minimize additives and chemicals. Some food manufacturers provide "cleaner" foods than others, and some manufacturers provide foods both with and without additives. Recently, I was asked to purchase corn chips for a family gathering. I read the ingredient labels on two competing brands: one listed "whole corn, corn oil, salt" and the other listed dozens of ingredients including chemicals, dyes, and monosodium glutamate (MSG). I purchased the chips with no additives or chemicals. They tasted great!

Avoid high fructose corn syrup (HFCS). Despite the manufacturers' advertising that it is natural because it is made from corn, HFCS is highly processed using chemicals. Manufacturers use HFCS because it is inexpensive (corn production is heavily subsidized in the United States), it tastes similar to sugar, and it is a preservative. Many health experts agree that this is a very bad food. Research shows that eating it shuts down satiety — even if you have eaten enough food your body doesn't get the message and you continue to eat. HFCS has been linked with obesity, fatty liver disease, and hypertension. The manufacturers' response has been to change the name to "corn sugar." HFCS is in many but not all manufactured foods. Read labels and compare products.

Eat organic. A teenaged client asked me, "Why do people choose non-organic — why would they intentionally eat food grown with chemical bug killers, mold inhibitors, and chemical fertilizers?" Why, indeed! Eating organic reduces your personal chemical load and reduces the flow of chemicals into the environment. Choosing organic supports sustainable agricultural practices. Eating organic also tastes better.

Avoid soy. Yes, this was widely touted as a health food for years. If you live or travel in the United States, 95% of all soy is genetically modified (GM), which means that it is substantially different than soy used to be. The safety of this new food has not been subject to multi-year testing. (GM foods are banned in many other nations because testing is not complete.) Nutritionists, gastroenterologists, and holistic doctors will tell you that many people are allergic or sensitive to soy. Many people with wheat or gluten sensitivity also are sensitive to soy.

In the United States, soy is one of the most heavily subsidized crops, which makes it very inexpensive. Like other beans, soy is high in protein. Many manufacturers add soy to their foods to increase protein levels. Unlike other beans, soybeans are up to 40% fat and because soybeans are so inexpensive in the United States, manufacturers have developed procedures for extracting oil from the bean. Soy oil is widely used for frying, is commonly found in "vegetable oil" and in "oil blends" in the United States, and is an ingredient in many manufactured foods.

Specific Foods – Eat This, Not That

When you have a choice between butter and something that looks like butter, choose the butter, preferably organic butter, and avoid the trans fats. In fact, if you can avoid margarine, do so. For cooking and salad dressings, olive oil is the time-tested healthy choice. Nuts and seeds provide excellent sources of protein and fat. I recommend low or no salt types. (Salted ones provide too much salt; if you eat them, you may find yourself with a dry mouth and possibly constipation.) One-eighth to one-quarter cup of nuts or seeds equals one portion. Roasted nuts and seeds are more easily digested than raw ones. Nuts and seeds are "real" foods and a vastly superior snack when compared to chips and processed foods. Most supply a balance of protein, fat, and carbohydrate as well as minerals. Eat sunflower seeds, pumpkin seeds, and all nuts except peanuts. Why no peanuts? A VERY high percentage of people are allergic to them. Also, aflatoxin, a toxic mold, is common on peanuts. NOTE: If you're going to eat peanuts, choose organic ones that have been tested for aflatoxin — check the label. When choosing between vegetables that are white or brown or vegetables that have color, make the more colorful choice.

When choosing among fresh, dried, or cooked fruit, choose fresh. Fresh fruit will have more nutrients. But, choose cooked when water is not pure and you cannot peel the fruit and choose cooked or dried when temperatures are low (in coat-wearing weather).

Food Sensitivities

Food sensitivities are a reality for most people today whether we recognize them or not! Many foods have been hybridized, some have been genetically modified, some are processed using toxic chemicals or heavy metals, and some are grown with toxins to fight mold, bacteria, viruses, or parasites. Simply speaking, we are eating foods today that previously did not exist. While most of us can tolerate some of these changes, most of us do not tolerate them all. Our bodies rebel, with reflux, rashes, constipation, diarrhea, stomach aches, joint aches, heart pain, headaches, and acne.

A good friend returned from a wonderful trip to Italy with his family. Unfortunately, he spent much of his time with terrible stomach cramps, diarrhea, and acid reflux that resulted in a cough in the middle of the summer. Surprisingly, he seemed better his first day back home. What dreaded disease did he have? He saw his family doctor, who quickly discovered my friend ate a large portion of gelato (ice cream), a food he didn't eat at home, every day of his trip. The doctor's advice: "You are sensitive to milk, don't eat ice cream." Without ice cream or milk, the symptoms stopped.

Food sensitivities are extremely common and even a small amount of a food to which you are sensitive can generate symptoms. Symptoms may include stomach ache, coughing, difficulty breathing, difficulty thinking, rashes, joint or muscle pain, and diarrhea. If YOU have symptoms, consider the list that follows of common food allergens. If you are eating a food you do not ordinarily have and it is on this list, discontinue for a few days and note any changes. (Food reactions may be delayed for several days, so exercise patience).

If you have a food sensitivity, *carry Allergy Restaurant Cards.* Available on-line, in different languages, these business card sized cards describe your sensitivity and how to avoid it. Order multiple copies in every language that you expect to encounter. In restaurants, provide a card to your server and ask that it be loaned to the cook. I love these cards and carry them everywhere!

FOOD

Common Food Allergies

Gluten — includes wheat, barley, oats (non-gluten-free), spelt, triticale. Contained in the vast majority of baked (bread, crackers, cookies, cake, pie) and fried goods, breakfast cereals, lunch meats, and in many sauces and soups. Contained in most soy sauce. Typically in meatloaf and meatballs and in many casseroles. Contained in beer (barley or wheat). Contained in many "seasoning blends," which may be applied in restaurants to flavor food. It's my experience that wheat is poorly tolerated by most people. It raises blood sugar higher than table sugar and is a major source of food cravings, neurological problems, joint pain, rashes, skin blisters, anxiety, reflux and many other digestive woes.

Dairy — includes milk from any mammal but especially from cows. Contained in ice cream, cream, many soups and sauces, many casseroles, and many baked goods. May result in increased mucus, sinus issues, post-nasal drip, abdominal pain, diarrhea, or constipation.

Soy — includes soy oil (common for frying foods, salad dressings, mayonnaise, corn chips), soy protein (in many protein bars, protein shakes, gluten-free products to increase protein content), soy flour (in gluten-free baked goods), soy sauce, sauces containing soy sauce, edamame, and soy lecithin (usually but not always well-tolerated). Soy is a highly allergenic food and many people who are sensitive to another food also are sensitive to soy.

Common Food Allergies, continued

FOOD

Corn — includes HFCS (high fructose corn syrup, which may be bad for all of us), corn syrup, corn oil or margarine, honey (when made with corn syrup), cornmeal, cornstarch, grits, spoon bread, corn bread, poultry or pork stuffing, whole, creamed or cut corn, many sodas. Many sauces and gravies. Chinese food. Corn is a very common sweetener.

Peanuts — found in peanut butter, some cookies, some sweets, some entrees. Sensitivity to peanuts can be severe, leading to anaphylaxis and even death. They are a legume, similar to soybeans.

Tree nuts — these are nuts that grow on trees and include walnuts and pecans.

Eggs — found in pastas, many baked goods including cookies, cakes, and pretzels, in many ice creams and puddings. Some vaccines.

Red Foods — especially shellfish (shrimp, scallops, lobster, crawfish), tomatoes, strawberries. Think of red and fire — inflammation.

MSG — not a food, but contained in many foods as an inexpensive flavor enhancer and meat tenderizer. Common cause of headaches, migraine, and foggy thinking.

People may be sensitive to foods that are not on this list, but the list covers the majority of food sensitivities. Chances are, if you are sensitive, the offending food is something on the list.

Pack Your Own Food

FOOD

My mother, who loves to travel, just asked me, "So, what SHOULD I pack? Am I stuck with carrying baggies full of banana chips?" Actually, unsweetened banana chips provide a good alternative to many snack foods, and I advised Mom to carry them. Luckily, she can find many other foods to eat during her travels.

The key to selecting packable travel food is finding nutritious food that is easily packed, easily prepared, and slow to spoil. Years ago, I carried dehydrated potato flakes, parboiled rice, instant oatmeal, instant grits, dried fruit, and a little beef jerky— I was so proud to have those! That was what was available for travel 30 to 40 years ago — minimal protein, no fat, and mainly starchy carbohydrates. No wonder I felt tired! It was easily packed, easily prepared, and slow to spoil. But I did not feel well eating it because it did not provide the nutrients I need.

Today, many foods that are suitable for travel are also nutritious. Thanks to advances in vacuum packaging and dehydration and improved distribution, we have many excellent travel food choices. You can eat well on the road, out of your pack or suitcase.

Carry leak-proof containers and bags for storage and mixing, and lightweight utensils. I recommend that you also carry an immersion heater or a hot pot to boil water, or a Jet Boil if you will be camping.

Carry high quality protein with you. For packable meat, poultry, and fish, check the supermarket. You can find salmon, tuna, and chicken in soft-sided vacuum packages that require no refrigeration and are good for months. (Carry small condiment packages for added flavor.) I always bring these with me, especially in carry-on luggage on planes. Beef and other meat jerky require no refrigeration and come in travel-sized soft packages; choose organic when you can. String cheese, available in many supermarkets, comes in individually wrapped portions and stays good for weeks. Hard and aged cheeses provide protein and fat and will stay good for days: carry them in a leak-proof container because they will grease up your gear. You can pack "instant" dehydrated beans that cook up quickly with boiling water. Plan to add dehydrated onions, carrots, and spices for flavor. Dehydrated beans are available in natural food stores, online, and in some supermarkets. Dehydrated soups are available in packages and sometimes in bulk in natural food stores and in some supermarkets. They cook up quickly with boiling water — carry a thermos with you for easy preparation. Hard boiled eggs are easy to carry, but are considered safe only for 2 hours unrefrigerated.

Sometimes, particularly for extended journeys, prepackaged processed food will be very helpful. Dehydrated powdered whey protein packs easily, comes in individual packets, and mixes with water to provide a protein boost. Try it before you travel — some brands taste better than others! I like bringing high quality *protein bars or meal replacement bars* with me for extended travel. Protein bars have the advantage of easy packability and they stay fresh for long periods. Look for bars made from real food (such as nuts and fruit) and without chemicals and preservatives. (If you can't pronounce the name of an ingredient, it likely is not good for you.) Make sure that your protein bar has enough protein to make a difference for you; I look for bars with at least 14 grams of protein per serving and whole fruit sweeteners. I don't buy bars that contain artificial sweeteners such as aspartame or saccharine, ever. I consider those substances dangerous, and I refuse to eat them.

Rotate your foods. If you have 2 kinds of fish, don't eat the same one every day or you will find yourself

113

tired of it quickly. The same thing goes for nuts or any other food — change your choices from day to day.

Plan to have high quality fats — you need them! Nuts and seeds pack easily and stay fresh for weeks at a time. Some people like to travel with a jar of nut butter — unopened nut butter stays good at room temperature for 18 or more months, opened nut butter will be good for weeks at a time. Toss it if it begins to smell rancid or "off." Consider packing individually sized nut butter packets, available at health food stores and online. Pack a small container of olive oil for drizzling on salads and vegetables.

Like chocolate? *High quality very dark chocolate* is a food that will nourish you, body and soul, and is a healthy source of fat. Choose chocolate that is at least 70% cocoa (preferably higher). Very dark chocolate has less sugar. Read the label and choose chocolate that is made with cocoa butter, not with a (less expensive and less healthy) substituted fat. Chocolate melts easily, so beware if you are traveling during high temperature times. If you choose to bring chocolate, bring extra! You may need to share.

Whole radishes, small cucumbers, and cut up carrots and celery make great travel food for plane rides or short car trips. An increasing variety of freeze-dried vegetables have become available in natural food and specialty food shops. Freeze-dried green beans, corn, and peas are all tasty. Small fruits, including apples, pears, tangerines, and plums, travel well on short trips. **Caution: In areas where tap water quality is uncertain, stick to fruit you peel yourself (do not eat the peel!) or wash and soak the fruit first in pure (bottled or boiled) water to which you have added 10–20 drops of grapefruit seed extract (GSE).** A potent but digestible antiseptic, grapefruit seed extract is available at health food stores.

FOOD

Unsweetened juices provide a healthy snack in moderation — consider one cup of juice as the rough equivalent of one piece of fruit. Limit juice intake to 1 cup per day. **Caution: Although fresh, non-pasteurized juices provide outstanding nutrition, insist on pasteurized juice for people with compromised immune systems.** Dried fruit, including prunes, figs, dates, cranberries, banana chips, pineapple, and raisins travel well on long trips but are higher in sugar. Limit your portion to ¼ cup daily!

Bring your own water. If water is convenient, you are more likely to stay hydrated. Convenient water displaces less healthy drink choices like highly sweetened soda. For air travel, I purchase a liter of water after I pass security and carry that with me on the plane. Why not use the airline's water? The airline doesn't give you enough! At out of town conferences I purchase a gallon of water at a supermarket or pharmacy and bring that to my hotel for drinking in the room and for refilling my water bottle. If you will be camping or will be in an area where water is not safe, bring a water filter, available at camping stores.

Eating in Restaurants

Many travelers choose fast food restaurants to save time and money when traveling, but consider this scenario. You choose your food while standing in a line that moves too slowly and place your order with a bored, indifferent, or impatient server. You eat your food, likely high in damaged fats, starch, salt, and sugar, as quickly as possible, dump the remains in the trash, and rush back to your car. We don't have to travel this way. We can eat better and feel better during travel. We can enjoy ourselves much more when we make a few changes to how we eat on the road.

115

FOOD

The key to selecting travel food lies in making the best choices among alternatives. If you are eating in a fast food restaurant, consciously choose to make healthier choices. Eat food in as close to its whole form as possible. Say NO to fried food. When possible, reduce added fat, chemicals, sugar, and salt and increase the fiber.

As a general rule, the less processed, the greater the nutritional value. Given the choice, *always choose the less processed food*. Choose eggs, meat, and a vegetable for breakfast, instead of bread or pancakes. If you must have starch, choose whole or steel-cut oats over instant oats, choose brown rice over white rice. Breads, particularly highly processed white bread or white sandwich rolls, are not a substitute for fruits or vegetables. Most dry cereal is highly processed, highly sugared, and contains little nutrition other than powdered vitamins. Skip it. If you eat yogurt, plain yogurt and fresh fruit make a great breakfast. Add seeds, coconut, or nuts to boost the protein and healthy fat. You say you have to have pancakes at least once on your trip? Insist on real maple syrup and real butter and order an egg on the side to boost the protein.

What about the bun or bread? Toss it! We are not talking about high quality breads that sustain life! These are highly salted and sugared flour-foods that have been stripped of fiber. Often, the bread is smeared with damaged fat in the form of highly allergenic soy or corn oil. Many people find that they feel more awake if they skip the roll or the bread! Some find that they are less prone to stomach upsets. Try it. If you must have bread, try to limit yourself to one time per week as a special treat and go for a wonderful croissant.

Go for the salad. (But avoid salad in areas where water quality is an issue.) Salad is a great choice, but avoid lunchmeat (ham, salami, etc.). Lunchmeat can be sky high in nitrites, salt, and other additives. Instead of a salad dressing with mystery ingredients, ask for olive oil and vinegar or lemon.

Do look for more vegetables. If an entree "comes with" rice or potatoes, ask the server to substitute vegetables — they often will for no charge. In Chinese or Thai restaurants, ask for an extra "$1 or $2 of broccoli" or of any other vegetable that they serve. In some places you will be limited to lettuce and tomato. Ask for an additional portion and expect to pay for it. Order side dishes of vegetables; you will feel better if you avoid the rice and noodles.

I am on strike against coffee creamers or "whiteners" that list anything but milk or cream. Most consist of soy or corn oil combined with a long chemical list. I would rather drink my coffee black or switch to tea.

If you want chicken and have a choice between grilled chicken or breaded and fried chicken, choose the grilled. (The cook likely uses trans fats or highly allergenic soy oil in the deep fat fryer.) If you have a choice between fried chopped and formed chicken or fried whole pieces of chicken, choose the whole pieces. If you want to have fish and the only choice is breaded and fried, feel free to scrape off the breading and eat the fish. *Avoid ground meat in restaurants* (meatballs, meatloaf, hamburger). Generally speaking, chopped meat is riskier (more likely to be contaminated) and of poorer quality. It's worth the extra expense to purchase a steak, stew, or chop.

Consider traveling a little farther off the highway to find restaurants that serve more than just fast food. *Look for places that cook food to order.* Local, non-chain restaurants sometimes provide "home cooking" that includes locally grown produce. Look for breakfast restaurants at any time of day. Breakfast and pancake restaurants typically serve "cooked to order" eggs,

117

FOOD

meats, and vegetables; I recommend that you skip the bread, pancakes, and waffles. Barbecue restaurants often have roasted meat and poultry and may have locally grown vegetable sides.

Ask a local! When possible, ask local people for restaurant recommendations. Generally, people love to talk about food, especially to visitors. I have found otherwise hidden treasures this way — you can too!

Check social media. Websites and apps such as Yelp can steer you to restaurants close to your location that have received good reviews, and they can warn you of poor quality. Specialty websites and apps list restaurants for people with particular food sensitivities. Online, Google or search for "gluten free" (or "soy free," etc.) and "restaurant" and the name of the city.

Foraging for Food at the Airport

Good luck. Many airlines no longer serve food, even on 4 or 5 hour flights, but they invite you to bring your own food on the plane. Finding real food at the airport can be a challenge. Many experienced travelers pack their own and supplement with beverages. Plan to purchase your water after you clear security; bringing more than 3½ ounces of any liquid is prohibited in the United States and in other nations. Avoid sweet or starchy snack foods in your quest for real and healthy food. You can almost always find nuts, dried fruit, and dark chocolate in airport shops. Look for fresh fruit and for cheese that you can eat or carry with you. Skip the yogurt if it is sweetened with artificial sweeteners or high fructose corn syrup.

Rarely, you may find specialty shops with dried meats and smoked fish — these can be wonderful for your trip. A made-to-order sandwich restaurant may be willing to provide you with a "no bread" sandwich on salad greens. Combine this with a piece of fruit for a quick and tasty meal. Many airport restaurants and take-out locations have a variety of salads; these may be your best choice if you are avoiding gluten, corn, soy, or dairy. If you are eating gluten free, be certain the croutons are individually packaged, away from your salad. Don't forget condiments and cutlery!

Off the Beaten Path

If you are traveling in areas where water is considered unsafe, or if you hear that travelers get diarrhea, assume that non-bottled water contains pathogens. Do not drink it unless it has been purified. Do not use ice! (Even on the plane.) Use only bottled water or other bottled beverages to brush your teeth or to rinse. Bring a water filter and iodine pills if bottled or boiled water will be unavailable.

When it comes to fruit and vegetables, "Peel it, Boil it, or Toss it." Do not eat salad. Do not eat the garnish on your plate. Do not eat tomatoes unless they have been cooked.

Bring your own knife for peeling.

FOOD

Food Summary

Eat real food:

- Close to original form and traditionally prepared.
- Real food spoils. Eat it before it does.
- Eat enough protein.
- Eat dairy if you can digest it.
- Choose colorful carbohydrates. Avoid white and brown.
- Limit sugar and starch.
- Avoid grain-based products, fried food, trans fats, chemicals and additives, and HFCS (high fructose corn syrup).
- Eat organic.
- Avoid soy.

Food sensitivities:

- Extremely common.
- Tiny amounts of food can trigger.
- Carry allergy restaurant cards.

Pack your own food:

- Easy to pack, easy to prepare, slow to spoil.
- Carry leakproof containers for storage and mixing.
- Carry lightweight utensils.
- Hot pot, immersion heater, or Jet Boil.
- Vacuum packed salmon, tuna, chicken, jerky.
- Carry condiments: mayonnaise, ketchup, hot sauce, mustard, relish.
- String and hard cheeses.
- Dehydrated beans and soups.
- Hard boiled eggs.

Food Summary, continued

- Whey protein powder (individual packs).
- Protein or meal replacement bars.
- Nuts and seeds.
- Nut butter packets.
- Dark chocolate.
- Whole radishes, cucumbers, carrots, celery.
- Freeze-dried vegetables.
- Small fruits: apples, pears, tangerines, plums.
- Dried fruit.
- Water.

Eating in restaurants:

- Choose less processed food.
- Skip the bread, cereal, and potatoes.
- Substitute vegetables for rice, noodles, and bread.
- Choose whole foods.
- Choose grilled instead of fried foods.
- Choose whole pieces of meat and poultry and avoid chopped meat.
- Travel off the highway to find local restaurants.
- Seek local recommendations for restaurants.
- Check social media for reviews.

Foraging for food at the airport:

- Pack your own and supplement with purchased beverages.

Off the beaten path:

- Assume non-bottled water is unsafe.
- Do not use ice.
- Peel it, Boil it, or Toss it: Rule for vegetables and fruit.
- No salad, no garnishes.
- Bring your own knife.

121

FOOT PROBLEMS

Years ago as a courtroom attorney, I wore the "uniform": navy blue suit, pumps with 2-inch heels, stockings. Although I lived in Atlanta, I was representing my Washington, D.C. client in a case in Orange County, California. The day before our trial, I awakened at 6 a.m., went for a run, changed into the "uniform," and was at work by 8. Still wearing stockings and heels, I met my client at the airport. (What was I thinking?) Like everyone else, we walked the mile in the airport to our plane. We flew to Dallas, where we had a two-hour layover and changed planes. We walked the mile to the next plane, me still in stockings and heels, and flew to LAX. Upon arrival we walked through the airport to baggage claim, dragged our luggage to ground transportation, and stood in line for the rental car. (My swollen feet!) We drove over an hour to our Orange County destination. By now, my swollen feet were on fire and my shoes were cutting into my feet. I was afraid to take off my shoes in the car — what if I couldn't get them back on? We arrived at the federal courthouse and admired the beautiful and incredibly hard marble floors. Every step hurt. We walked (why wasn't I wearing sneakers?) to the file clerk's office and stood in line. Then we walked to the judge's office and waited, standing, for a clerk. I could barely concentrate.

I was wearing very sensible shoes that were well broken-in. Selbys. Navy blue, medium heel, wide toe. It didn't matter. By the end of the day all I could think of was the pain. When I finally got to my hotel room I gently tried to remove my shoes. They didn't budge. I looked. My feet were bulging and gripping the shoes. I wrenched one shoe off and quickly began massaging my swollen and aching foot. (Why do we wear these things?!?) There were deep creases where the shoe cut me. The creases burned. My arches ached.

Today, older and wiser, you couldn't pay me to wear heels all day long through three airports and on two planes. Wearing heels or any tight or ill-fitting shoes will guarantee aching feet on an extended trip. Given the right conditions, even comfortably clad feet will swell and hurt.

General Sore Feet Advice

Avoid getting sore feet. Assume that you will walk more than usual when traveling so wear comfortable shoes with adequate support. Shoes that pinch, bind, rub, or squeeze do not qualify — leave them at home. If you need such shoes for your job or a special event, carry them and change your shoes after you arrive.

Wear the recommended footgear for your travel. I still remember the woman at the bottom of the Grand Canyon with the most amazing blisters. She had hiked down the day before wearing sandals. SANDALS! The recommended footgear was heavy duty hiking boots with two pairs of socks. Needless to say, she couldn't hike anywhere! (Wearing sandals, she also risked twisting an ankle, sunburn, and snake, scorpion, and other bites.) She was lucky, all she had was blisters. She eventually was airlifted out of the canyon at tremendous expense (to her).

If you wear special shoe inserts or insoles, be sure to bring them and wear them. Magnetic insoles, available in drug stores, natural food stores, and through the Nikken company, reduce foot fatigue and aches for many people. I think they are great! Cushioned insoles, which are very inexpensive and available at drugstores and supermarkets, can help.

Keep your feet dry. Travel often entails keeping our shoes on for longer periods of time, and our feet don't

123

air out. Be aware that your feet sweat. To keep your feet drier, air your feet at regular intervals. To absorb added moisture, powder your feet with cornstarch. Cornstarch is available in food markets and in pharmacies as an ingredient in foot or baby powder. Keeping your feet dry will reduce the likelihood of hot spots, blisters, and athlete's foot. When camping, many people keep their socks on even after removing their shoes. The socks retain moisture and the feet stay damp. If you feel the need to constantly wear socks, when you remove your shoes first dry your feet, then powder them, and put on clean, dry socks.

Use moleskin. Stick self-adhesive moleskin on spots that normally become sore to prevent blistering. When walking, hiking, or trekking, STOP and apply moleskin as soon as you feel a sore or hot spot developing — you will avoid most blisters this way.

Try professionally fitted shoes. If you chronically suffer from sore and aching feet, your shoes may not fit! Schedule an appointment at an athletic shoe shop that specializes in fitting. Find a store that will analyze your arch—standing and sitting—and analyze your gait using video. The right shoe for you will feel great!

Elevate your feet. Placing your feet above the level of your heart puts gravity to work for you. You can reduce swelling at no expense and your feet will feel so much better. Raising your feet even a little will help soothe tired feet. When you anticipate a long day or when your feet already hurt, use a footrest. On plane trips, arrange your under-seat luggage or pillows to create a footrest and place your feet on top. It will help.

Massage your feet with a ball. Sure, I'd love to have a massage therapist nurture my feet, but that is not always convenient. Take any small ball — a golf ball or tennis ball, for example. Place it under your foot and apply pressure to it while rolling it back and forth and around. Don't press so hard that you bruise yourself. Within moments your foot will begin to tingle. Continue your massage for a few seconds more and switch feet. Ahhh.

Get a professional pedicure before you travel. A friend does this prior to all trips, and she swears by it! The pedicurist trims and shapes all the nails, softens calluses, and finishes with a foot massage. Nail color is included. (I'm thinking about this for my next trip....)

Get reflexology. Reflexology is a form of bodywork that focuses on the feet, hands, and sometimes the ears to promote general health. It also is invaluable for promoting foot health and comfort. I use it when preparing for major treks. It increases my general health level, improves my sleep, and makes my feet feel great.

Herbs

Several years ago I attended my nephew's bar mitzvah with my parents at a beautiful country inn in rural New Hampshire. It was the end of a long day and my father, the original party animal, was moving slowly and wincing. I pulled him aside and he reluctantly told me that he had left his prescription diuretic, Lasix, at home. He pulled up his pants legs — his ankles were swollen like melons! He was afraid to take off his shoes because he was certain he'd never get them back on. We were miles away from the nearest store. He agreed to try an herb — anything to reduce the swelling.

I follow a simple rule in cases like this; "The herb you need is in your own backyard" (or in the kitchen or on the hotel grounds). I went outside for a walk. Dandelion plants were everywhere, and within moments I had a handful of *dandelion leaf*. I rinsed the leaf in the bathroom sink, tore it into small pieces and crushed it with a spoon inside Dad's room mug. I added boiling

125

water from the kitchen, steeped it for 5 minutes, stirred, and gave Dad his tea. Fifteen minutes later, he grinned and walked to the bathroom. He drank about 4 mugs per day, was able to delay using Lasix until he returned home, and eliminated his ankle swelling.

Interestingly, when we returned to my parents' home in New Jersey, I noticed the weed plantain was growing everywhere. Plantain is another excellent diuretic that can be prepared the same way as dandelion leaf. The herb Dad needed really does grow in his yard.

If you are retaining water, you may wish to take 1 dropperful of dandelion leaf tincture (not the root) or 1 teaspoon of the tea steeped or simmered in 1 cup of water for 5 minutes, 3 times per day. You may wish to gather your own fresh leaf and drink the tea like my father did. It will send you to the bathroom, so be sure to continue drinking your water. Dandelion leaf is a remarkable diuretic because it is so gentle and so effective. It even contains its own potassium.

Sometimes your feet ache and you want to put something on them. *Witch hazel* is an excellent, astringent remedy that relieves sore and achy feet. Buy witch hazel liquid from the drugstore or natural food store and apply it directly to those aching feet. Use enough to moisten the skin, rub it in, and let your feet and ankles air dry. Long term daily use will shrink varicose veins — it really works!

You say you don't have any witch hazel? Soak your feet in *ginger tea*. Ginger's mildly stimulating effect gets your foot fluids moving, thereby relieving swelling and pain. Another good foot bath choice is *Epsom salts*. Dissolve a cup of Epsom salts in 1–2 quarts of hot water and soak your feet in the solution. Add 1–2 drops of peppermint or lavender essential oil to the foot bath for a spa-like experience.

Homeopathics

Homeopathic *Arnica*, 6c or 30c taken internally, 1 pellet beneath your tongue, or *Arnica gel or cream* smoothed on your feet reduces soreness. **Caution: Don't use Arnica externally on broken skin.** Take 1 pellet at the beginning of your travel day to reduce swelling and pain. Take up to 3 times a day for foot pain, and feel free to use both the internal and external forms.

If you get swollen feet and Arnica just isn't enough, you might want to try homeopathic witch hazel, *Hamamelis*, potency of 6c to 30c. Take 1 pellet at the beginning of the day and repeat this dose for a total of up to 3 times per day. In addition, you may take this remedy 3 times in an hour spaced every 20 minutes to reduce the pain of aching feet. If your feet are red, swollen, and painful, another excellent choice is homeopathic *Apis*. Take as directed for homeopathic Hamamelis. See "Choosing Homeopathic Remedies," page 21.

Make your own external application! For a soothing foot wash or foot bath, dissolve a pellet of homeopathic Arnica, Hamamelis, or Apis in 1–2 cups of water, stir rapidly until dissolved, and either soak your feet in the water or soak a washcloth in the water and apply it to your feet. Instant relief!

Essential Oils

Essential oils are the BEST when it comes to feet! One drop of *peppermint essential oil* in cool water makes a refreshing foot bath for hot and aching feet. **(Caution: If you are on constitutional homeopathic treatment, skip the peppermint or any product that contains or smells of camphor.)** Try a *lavender essential oil* compress by adding 5 drops of the oil to a moistened handkerchief and massage upwards from your feet to your calves. This is a great remedy for airline foot swelling, and you can do it on the plane.

127

Food Choices for Sore or Swollen Feet

If your swollen feet are the result of simple water retention, *stop eating salt!* This can be difficult when traveling because so many prepared foods are made with large amounts of salt, but you can reduce salt consumption by putting down the salt shaker. Also, avoid eating high-salt foods such as salted nuts, salty chips, nachos, canned soups, canned tomato juice, and many sauces. Salad is great, but the salad dressing can be loaded with salt as well as with sugar (which also increases water retention!) so order dressing on the side, limit your dressing portion to half and toss the rest, or dress your salad yourself with oil and vinegar or lemon. Increase your consumption of water to flush your system and reduce water retention.

Like my dad discovered, *dandelion leaf*, which grows almost everywhere and is available in some areas as a salad or cooked green, is a potent diuretic that will reduce swelling. *Nettles*, which may be cooked in soup as a green or simmered in water for 20 minutes for tea, is another natural diuretic. Pick your own (but wear gloves, nettles sting until dried or cooked!). Or find nettle leaf tea in bulk or in bags at a natural food store. *Watermelon* fruit, or a tea made from a handful of the seeds simmered in 2 cups of water for 20 minutes, also will clear excess water. Drink ½ cup 4 times per day.

Athlete's Foot, Fungus, and Yeast

A friend's daughter had a college semester abroad in a semi-wilderness area in Central America. The daughter called home and said she would be sent home if she could not heal her feet. She had a terrible case of foot fungus with red peeling and oozing skin. She had difficulty walking and was in pain. She could not identify the local plants, could not travel to a pharmacy, and was prohibited from seeing the local medicine man.

What could she do?

She could use *vinegar*! Vinegar is available around the world and is inexpensive.

My friend's daughter did an all-day vinegar bath, wearing plastic bags on her feet filled with vinegar and tied at the ankle with bandanas. She drank vinegar water at every meal. She changed her socks 3 times per day, washed them daily, and dried them in full sunshine. After the first day, she did daily foot soaks in vinegar. She felt better the first day and continued to improve. She completed her overseas studies, comfortably.

Athlete's foot, fungus, and yeast—when on the feet—are three ways of saying the same thing. These are common problems for many people that are exacerbated by travel. Yeast thrives on dampness so if your feet stay damp you are inviting yeast. Keep your feet dry with *cornstarch* and read the suggestions under "General Sore Feet Advice" in this chapter. If you have or tend to get athlete's foot, consider adding *baking soda* or *garlic powder* to your foot powder! Both eliminate yeast.

Like my friend's daughter, you can use vinegar! Pour vinegar into a large bowl or small tub and soak your feet in it for at least 5 minutes daily. For quicker results, wrap your foot in a plastic bag filled with vinegar — the portable vinegar bath — and wear the bag for up to 24 hours. (Do the day-long bath only one time — repeated use can leach calcium from your body.) To speed the process, also take vinegar internally. Try to purchase apple cider vinegar — it is better for you and it is tasty. The dose is 1 teaspoon 3 times per day before meals, taken in one-third cup of water. The combined internal and external approach speeds your healing.

Cracking heels and torn skin between your toes are a sign of yeast. For relief, apply several drops of *tea tree oil* directly to your feet, full strength, 2–3 times per day.

129

Or soak a cotton ball in tea tree oil and tape it to the area overnight. If your feet are sensitive to tea tree oil, dilute it by placing 15 drops of tea tree oil in 1–2 teaspoons (5–10 ml) of olive oil or another food grade oil. Alternatively, apply several drops of *lavender* essential oil, full strength, 2–3 times per day. You're in a remote area and can't obtain essential oils? Mash several *garlic cloves* (even available in the wilderness), and apply full strength for 1–2 hours or combine with cooking or massage oil overnight and cover with a sock. Overnight, the garlic cure can reduce even stubborn fungus problems, but full strength garlic WILL burn your feet if left in place for more than a few hours! It also will give you the worst case of garlic breath! (Eating a large handful of parsley reduces garlic breath.) Follow the garlic cure by applying lavender essential oil directly to the affected area. (Ten to 20 drops will cover the entire sole of your foot.). A product available at some pharmacies called *Zinn's Crack Creme* helps heal cracked heels. Apply 2 times daily.

Yellow or opaque fingernails or toenails are a sign of yeast overgrowth. Apply a few drops of tea tree oil directly to the nail and the nail bed at least 2 times per day. This works remarkably well, especially when combined with an internal remedy (see below).

Know that foot fungus can be stubborn — it takes time to grow a new nail — and plan on continuing treatment for at least 6 months. To improve your results and reduce treatment time, treat yourself internally as well as externally. *Pau d'arco* is a tasty herb with outstanding anti-fungal qualities. Take 1 dropperful of the tincture 3 times per day or drink 1 cup of tea 3 times per day, made by simmering 3 tablespoons of herb in 4 cups of water for 30 minutes. Enjoy!

Grapefruit seed extract (GSE) taken internally, 1 capsule or 10 drops internally 3 times per day, will help.

For external application, mix 1 teaspoon GSE with 1 teaspoon of vegetable oil, and apply directly to the feet.

Homeopathic *Nitric acid* 6c or 30c stands out as a remedy for skin cracks — take 1 pellet beneath your tongue 2 times per day for 3 days. If it is going to help, you will see good results within that time. If it is not working, stop and do something else. If it is working, take 1–2 doses daily as needed. If warm water makes your feet feel better, homeopathic *Arsenicum* 6c or 30c may be your remedy. Take as directed for homeopathic Nitric acid.

When it comes to foot fungus, or fungus anywhere in the body, natural remedies work as well or better than highly priced and sometimes toxic prescription medications. You just need to take them consistently.

Stinky Feet

Essential oils can help clear the smell from stinky feet. Two drops of *cypress or lemongrass essential oil* added to your foot powder will naturally deodorize your feet. The cypress essential oil also helps relieve sore and achy feet.

If your feet smell, your socks and your shoes also smell. Be sure to change your socks at least once a day. Powder your feet with *cornstarch and baking soda* and shake some into your shoes each day. The baking soda absorbs odor.

FOOT PROBLEMS

Foot Problems Summary

General sore feet advice:
- Wear comfortable shoes with inserts or insoles.
- Wear recommended footgear.
- Keep feet dry.
- Moleskin.
- Elevate your feet.
- Massage feet with a ball.
- Reflexology.
- Foot bath with Epsom salts.
- Use herbs: Dandelion leaf, witch hazel, nettle leaf, plantain leaf, ginger tea.
- Try homeopathic remedies: Arnica, Hamamelis, Apis.
- Use essential oils: Peppermint or cypress essential oil.
- Avoid salt.

Fungus and cracked skin:
- Vinegar.
- Tea Tree or lavender essential oil.
- Garlic.
- Grapefruit seed extract (GSE).
- Homeopathic Nitric acid or Arsenicum.
- Zinn's Crack Cream.

Stinky feet:
- Change socks daily.
- Powder with cornstarch and baking soda.

INDIGESTION

You've waited all year for this trip. You've planned for months, and read all the guidebooks, and now you have arrived at your destination. Your party is ready to explore, to find a great restaurant, or to just have fun. And YOU have a stomach ache. You feel ridiculous. You don't want to hold everyone back, you don't want to be the wet blanket in the group, but you really feel terrible. Everyone else is ready to rock and roll, and you would really rather sleep or watch TV and wait for your stomach to calm down.

Sound familiar? It is very common. At this point, slowing down and taking some time for yourself may be the best plan. It may not fit everyone's schedule, but it certainly could help you feel better.

Breathe. This is a great time to just sit and BREATHE. Breathe slowly, focusing on your stomach, imagining that you are breathing in and out of your stomach. Close your eyes if you can. Think the word "calm" or "relax" or "easy" as you breathe. Five to 10 minutes of quiet breathing may clear your indigestion, and certainly will help you feel better. Can't do this in front of your group? I often imagine that hotel restrooms are filled with travelers doing their breathing and relaxation exercises. Don't feel shy. No one knows that you are breathing behind your locked stall door.

Stop eating. This may be a good time to take a break from eating. See how you feel. If missing a meal makes you queasy, try eating very lightly. Avoid foods that inflame the digestive system: sugar, starch, alcohol, caffeine, chemicals, and all battered and deep fried foods. Try a little broth. Eat some yogurt or sip some kefir, but skip the unfermented milk. Eating lightly for 24 hours may be sufficient to eliminate your digestive woes.

INDIGESTION

Take a walk, do yoga, do tai chi. Sometimes we sit too long when we travel. Imagine a tube that is crimped in the middle. That "crimp" — the result of sitting to long in a car, train, or plane — interferes with digestion. Stretch and eliminate the crimp with gentle, regular movement combined with breathing. Taking a walk, doing some yoga, or playing tai chi — all will help.

Travelers' Remedies

Several friends and clients, upon reading this section, told me that I missed the point. They said that when we travel, we CONSCIOUSLY, intentionally over-indulge. They asked, rather pointedly, what they could take when they eat too much, drink too much, or generally indulge? For the hangover, heartburn, sour stomach, or acid indigestion caused by over-indulging, I recommend homeopathic *Nux vomica* 30c. It is amazing how well this works! Are you planning to drink and eat too much? Try taking 1 pellet of Nux to reduce the ill effects. Some friends who otherwise do not use homeopathy (they say they just don't believe in it) carry and use this remedy! Take 1 pellet every 15 minutes for 1 hour or until symptoms subside, repeating the dose as needed. See "Choosing Homeopathic Remedies," page 21.

Food and Herbal Remedies

Many excellent indigestion remedies are found in the kitchen. Know that in an emergency, you usually can find what you need in restaurant kitchens and food markets.

Vinegar is a fabulous indigestion remedy. One teaspoon stirred into a glass of water has cleared many cases of indigestion. I prefer apple cider vinegar (ACV), but any vinegar will do. Repeat as needed.

Yes, of course, ginger. *Ginger* candied, powdered, fresh, tinctured, or in tea — all forms are effective.

Getting ginger in any form into your system will help to settle your stomach. Ginger is my remedy of choice for stomach distress from flu, car or motion sickness, eating bad food, or poor food choices. I always carry a bottle of the tincture because it has so many other uses, such as warming me in frigid conference rooms and helping to fight a cold. While ginger is a very effective remedy, you may need frequent doses. Of the tincture, take 4–5 drop doses every 2–5 minutes until pain and nausea clear, and then take as needed. It is not unusual to experience immediate improvement and for your symptoms to return moments later! Just keep taking it.

You can use fresh ginger root from a kitchen or food market, gnawing off 1/16 teaspoon or more. The dose for capsules is 1 capsule, and the dose for powdered herb is 1/4 teaspoon, which can be swallowed with water or may be emptied into water and drunk for more rapid effect. Or slice 1–3 teaspoons of fresh ginger into 2 cups of water and simmer for 10 minutes to make a lovely tea that will halt nausea and settle the stomach. Sip slowly; the effects are powerful but short-lived.

Have you noticed that ALL sushi restaurants serve pickled ginger? They do, and for good reason! The Japanese and Chinese historically have used ginger as a primary antidote for "fish poison," meaning bad or tainted fish. (You would think that people who eat raw fish would suffer indigestion more often — perhaps they don't because of they combine every bite of sushi (and sashimi) with a slice of ginger!)

Speaking of sushi (and sashimi), *horseradish or wasabi* (a type of horseradish) also is an antidote for fish poison. (Isn't THAT interesting?) The Japanese traditionally serve horseradish with raw fish, eastern European Jews traditionally serve horseradish with gefilte fish, and Americans serve horseradish with roast

INDIGESTION

beef. Therapeutically, horseradish disperses stagnation. It keeps things moving and helps with digestion. While I don't carry horseradish with me, it is an excellent emergency medicine found in many homes, restaurants, and grocery stores. I recommend a teaspoon of grated or prepared (from a jar) horseradish — it is tasty on a cracker. One other great emergency use of horseradish is that it will enable you to urinate when you cannot. It also clears the sinuses and warms you when you feel chilled.

Fennel, a spice found in many kitchens, is a great remedy for indigestion. If you've ever been in an Indian restaurant, you likely passed a bowl of fennel seeds at the front door! Many patrons take a pinch or small handful of fennel and chew them on the way home. Fennel, eaten as seeds or powdered, in capsules, brewed as tea, or taken in tincture form, clears gas and bloating. I have watched friends who were doubled over with the pain of acute gas resume normal activities within 20 minutes of taking fennel. Fennel tastes like licorice. It is a wonderful remedy for pregnant or nursing moms because it increases mothers' milk. In fact, fennel taken by a nursing mom is an excellent remedy for her nursing child with colic.

Chamomile is THE herb of choice for indigestion linked to anger. Widely available in restaurants, food stores, and health food stores, chamomile is a well-known and tasty tea that contains no caffeine. Very mild, it is suitable for children, pregnant and nursing moms, and for people on a wide range of medications. Personally, I find that chamomile tea prepared from a single tea bag is only a pleasant beverage, not a remedy for indigestion. To settle your stomach, count on using no fewer than 2 tea bags or (even better) 1 tablespoon of dried chamomile herb for one cup of water. Steeping the tea 10–15 minutes brings out the healing qualities and increases the strength. I carry the 1 ounce tincture for travel — one dropperful does the trick and makes a tasty "instant" tea.

Chamomile tincture is a very fast, very effective remedy. On a recent camping trip with a friend and her 4-year-old daughter, the daughter got into the marsh-mallows before lunch of our last day. We had been planning to hike out that afternoon. Well, little Emily was holding her stomach and wasn't going ANYWHERE. We gave her 2 drops of chamomile tinc-ture and repeated the dose every 20 minutes. (Feeling impatient, I personally took a dropperful.) Emily stopped holding her stomach and visibly relaxed. (I felt more relaxed, too.) About an hour later, we had packed our tents and were on our way. We offered Emily more, but she said her tummy was fine. Success! For adults: 1–2 droppersful, every half hour until symptoms clear.

Catnip is one of my favorite herbs for indigestion, particularly when brought on by anxiety. A member of the mint family, it is tasty, gentle enough for young children, and very effective. Take 1 dropper of the tinc-ture every 15 minutes until the indigestion eases; 1 or 2 doses will provide great relief. A few drops on a piece of cloth or on a cat toy will greatly entertain your cat!

Have indigestion with a headache or with ulcer type pain? The herb *meadowsweet* helps with headaches, stomach pain, and ulcers. Take 1 dropperful, hourly or as needed. Or drink a tea made from 1 tablespoon of the dried herb steeped in 2 cups of recently boiled water. Drink ¼–½ cup every half hour.

Got oranges? Scrub, then peel an *orange or tanger-ine*, give the juicy fruit to a friend who does not have indigestion, and use the peel as an indigestion remedy. (Choose organic citrus if you have a choice.) Simmer the peel in 2 cups of water and sip for a tasty and effec-tive indigestion remedy.

Or try *bitters* for indigestion. Bitters refers to a variety of herbs or herbal combinations that taste bitter, stimulate digestion, and clear indigestion. Consider carrying bitters with you if you regularly experience indigestion. Many herbalists make their own bitters combinations, with herbs that may include gentian, dandelion root, yarrow, and yellow dock. (You can make a GREAT combination from 10 parts gentian root, 4 parts bitter orange peel, and 1 part cardamom. Add 1 part mugwort if you are dealing with parasites. Grind in a coffee grinder or blender, place in a jar, add 4 ounces of vodka for each ounce of dry bitters, label, shake daily for 2 weeks, and then strain.) Take 1–2 droppersful doses before meals or 1 dropperful every 15 minutes to clear indigestion — stir into water and drink.) A ready-made version is *Swedish Bitters*, found in health food stores. Find *Angostora Bitters*, containing herbal gentian, at bars and in liquor stores.

Umeboshi plum or umeboshi paste is a food that settles indigestion. Found in natural food stores in the macrobiotics section, this condiment is widely available in Japanese kitchens. Be prepared for the very salty taste! Take half teaspoon doses, hourly or until symptoms clear. Umeboshi has another, remarkable use: It will stop you or a child from crying — try it!

Homeopathic Remedies

Nux vomica 30c — described at the beginning of this chapter — provides relief from many forms of indigestion, but especially for the person who feels impatient and cold with indigestion or for indigestion brought on by over-indulgence. Try *Carbo veg* 30c for indigestion following over-indulgence if Nux vomica fails to help, especially if you feel gassy and weak and if you feel worse lying down. I recommend *Arsenicum album* 30c as the best general remedy for food poison-

138

ing. I also think of it anytime someone has bad stomach pain or indigestion with vomiting and/or diarrhea. (If Arsenicum does not provide immediate relief for food poisoning, try homeopathic *Veratrum album* 30c.)

Use homeopathic *Podophylum* 30c for indigestion with yellow stool that passes without pain. Homeopathic *Natrum phosphoricum* 6x or 30c (Nat phos) is a great "general" indigestion remedy that some people use as their "go to" solution. Take *Argentum nitricum* 30c (Arg nit) if your indigestion was brought on by eating too much sugar or if you struggle with performance anxiety. Take 1 pellet of any of the above every 15 minutes for up to 1 hour. Change remedies if you experience no improvement, and stop taking the remedy if your indigestion clears. (See "Homeopathic Remedies" in the chapter on Diarrhea for additional suggestions.)

Essential Oils

A good friend carries a small (5 ml) bottle of *peppermint essential oil* everywhere she goes. One drop (yes, only 1!) added to a glass of water helps settle the stomach. Its mild sedating effect on the stomach eliminates nausea. This is a WONDERFUL remedy that works for many people. It is easy to carry, smells nice, and works pretty well. Plus, there is plenty to share with all your friends. **Caution #1: Check with your homeopath first if you are receiving constitutional care; he or she may tell you this is not the remedy for you. Caution #2: Avoid use if you tend towards acid reflux or heartburn — it can make these problems worse.**

Another great essential oil for indigestion is *rosemary*. Stir 1 drop rapidly into a cup of water and sip. Be aware! Rosemary is stimulating and will wake you up! Got *lavender* essential oil? Rub 8 drops on your abdomen and smell your lavender scented hands. This remedy helps relieve anxiety-based indigestion.

Supplements

Do you have any *probiotics*, with names such as acidophilus, bifidus, and others? Take 1–2 capsules hourly until indigestion subsides. Probiotics may be taken on an empty or full stomach. Also, natural probiotics, found in *fermented foods* such as yogurt or kefir with live cultures, or in sauerkraut and kimchi, can greatly aid digestion.

One holistic physician highly recommends *digestive enzymes* for indigestion. Take 1 or 2 capsules as directed, during or immediately after eating. This is NOT the remedy to take, however, on an empty stomach!

Grapefruit seed extract (GSE) is my "go to" remedy if I am in an area where I suspect water contamination. In such areas I carry GSE in my pocket and take a capsule as soon as I feel any digestive discomfort. I'll also take it if I have no other remedy available as it is very effective for a wide range of physical (but not emotional) issues. Take 3 times per day and up to hourly for continued distress.

Pharmaceutical Remedies

When I was growing up in New Jersey, many diners ("greasy spoons," my father called them) sold Tums and Pepto Bismol at the cash register, next to the foot-high cakes, deep dish pies, and half-pound muffins. They knew people needed help digesting their food, which was high in sugar and starch and mostly deep fried. I don't recommend those remedies unless they are all you can find! Sometimes, you just have to compromise.

Indigestion in the Wilderness

Teas prepared from certain aromatic trees provide great wilderness remedies for indigestion. *Birch tree inner bark*, especially from black (sweet), yellow, or any birch inner bark that tastes like wintergreen, is an especially good remedy. To prepare the bark, prune a small branch from the tree, strip off the outer bark and then the inner bark. Simmer 1 tablespoon of the inner bark in 2 cups of water for 20 minutes. Drink half a cup of tea every 30 minutes. Chew on a small twig while you are waiting for the tea — and enjoy the wintergreen taste. *Sassafras* inner bark and root bark tea is amazingly tasty and settles the stomach. Use about a tablespoon of bark for 2 cups of water — you can rely on this as a remedy but not as an everyday beverage. *Evergreen trees* are your friends: use pine, juniper or thuja (*Arbor vitae*) needles/tips simmered in water for 20 or more minutes for a tasty stomach settling tea.

Kudzu root, from the "ornamental" vine imported from the Orient that now covers the southern United States, is a fabulous indigestion remedy. Use the root, which typically is large and very difficult to dig! Scrub or peel and shave, cut, or grate into small pieces. Simmer 1 tablespoon in 2 cups of water for 20 or more minutes.

Charcoal often clears indigestion. (See the section on "Diarrhea in the Wilderness" for how to prepare your own charcoal.)

INDIGESTION

Indigestion Summary

General Recommendations:
- Breathe.
- Fast for 12–24 hours.
- Eat lightly. Avoid inflammatory foods.

Move:
- Walk.
- Yoga.
- Tai chi.

Food and herbal remedies:
- Vinegar.
- Ginger.
- Horseradish and wasabi.
- Fennel seed.
- Chamomile.
- Catnip.
- Meadowsweet.
- Orange or tangerine peel.
- Bitters.

Homeopathic remedies:
- Nux vomica.
- Carbo veg.
- Arsenicum album.
- Veratrum album.
- Podophylum.
- Natrum phosphoricum.
- Argentum nitricum.

Indigestion Summary, continued

Essential oils:
- Peppermint.
- Rosemary.
- Lavender.

Supplements:
- Probiotics.
- Digestive enzymes.
- Grapefruit seed extract.

Pharmaceutical remedies:
- Tums.
- Pepto Bismol.

Indigestion in the wilderness:
- Birch tree.
- Sassafras tree.
- Evergreens: Pine, Juniper or Thuja.
- Kudzu root.
- Charcoal.

Top packable remedies:
- Nux vomica.
- Ginger capsules.
- Peppermint essential oil.
- Ginger candy, ginger capsules, or ginger tincture.
- Activated charcoal.

INSOMNIA

At the lecture, you couldn't keep your eyes open. Now, back in your hotel room, you can't fall asleep. Tomorrow is your big presentation — you need to be at your best, you finally have gone to bed, and you are wide awake. Or, exhausted from traveling, you lie down in bed and find yourself shaking and utterly unable to sleep.

Many of us are sensitive when it comes to sleep. We handle so many stresses in our lives, we accomplish so much, do so many things. But interfere with our sleep and our happiness, productivity, and sense of well-being disappear. We are more prone to colds and flu when our sleep is below par. Our endurance, strength, and focus diminish. We feel rotten!

Eliminate Stimulants

So what can we do? A good start is to reduce or eliminate those things that awaken or stress you during the evening.

Avoid caffeine in beverages. Foods that awaken you include all caffeine products: This means no coffee or tea with dinner. Caffeine sensitive people may need to eliminate caffeine after 12 noon! (By the way, decaffeinated teas and coffee still have caffeine — just less of it.) Green tea has caffeine. Many so-called herbal blend teas have caffeine; if the tea contains black tea or green tea, it has caffeine. Chamomile and mint teas, or teas with names like Sleepy Time or Nighty Night typically have no caffeine. Many soft drinks contain caffeine, especially colas, Mountain Dew, Surge, and Jolt! "Functional drinks" to increase energy or stamina, such as Red Bull, contain caffeine and other stimulants — that's why people use them to wake up. Read labels.

Avoid taking drugs that contain caffeine. Examine the labels of any drugs, especially over-the-counter drugs, to see if they contain caffeine. Drugs that commonly include caffeine are decongestants, weight loss products, painkillers, and products to relieve cramps, among others. Often, the amount of caffeine in one dose is equivalent to the caffeine in a cup of coffee! If you need a decongestant to sleep and your decongestant contains caffeine, it won't help you sleep. Many medications are available without caffeine — ask your pharmacist. Are you taking a product to boost your energy? They work, but they can keep you revved up far longer than you intended. Take them early in the day to avoid sleep interference. Pseudoephedrine, a pharmaceutical decongestant found in Sudafed and a number of other medications, can keep you awake. Read the label.

Avoid foods that keep you awake. The one piece of chocolate may not bother you, but that glorious "Death by Chocolate" dessert you ate at 11 p.m. may keep you awake for hours! High sugar and caffeine in that dessert may be the cause.

Certain liquors will keep you awake. Red wine keeps many people wide awake; white wine awakens fewer people. Also, be alert to liquors that put you to sleep but result in troubled sleep. Abstinence, reduced consumption, or a change to "cleaner" beverages such as vodka may help.

Eat Earlier to Improve Your Sleep

Eating late keeps many travelers awake. While traveling, there are so many things to do that we often are pulled far from our accustomed schedules. Instead of your accustomed 6 or 7 p.m. dinner, you may be eating at 9 or 10. Food can give you an energy boost that keeps you going for several more hours. How late you finish eating makes a big difference in how you sleep. If you are suffering from insomnia and are eating several hours later than your accustomed time, try eating earlier.

145

Increasing the foods that aid relaxation can assist with your sleep. As a rule, high carbohydrate foods are more sedating than protein or fat. Many healthy travelers carefully limit their consumption of carbohydrates during the day for energy or weight loss. Evening is the time to have a baked potato, rice, beans, or other high carbohydrate food. You don't need much; even a tablespoon of a high carbohydrate food helps with sleep. If you are going to eat a piece of bread today, have it with dinner.

Consuming foods high in tryptophan can help you sleep. In the United States, who can forget eating turkey at Thanksgiving and then watching or experiencing the stupor! That stupor comes partly from overeating and partly from the turkey, which is high in tryptophan. Other foods that are high in tryptophan include tuna, milk and yogurt, bananas, dates, figs, whole grains, and nut butters. Remember that glass of warm milk at bedtime? It can help you sleep. (But brush your teeth before going to bed!)

Quiet Time

Too much excitement experienced too late in the day can keep us awake. Have you gone to a late night concert, performed in a late sporting event, watched an emotional movie, surfed the Internet, or simply seen the late night news? What were you doing, what were you thinking, to engage in these activities within two hours of your proposed bedtime? If you were excited and it was late, sheer excitement can keep you awake. In this case, you want to *find a way to wind down* or schedule your fun earlier. (Yeah, right!) Deep breathing, slow repetitive movements, prayer or meditation, writing, or a warm bath may help.

Breathe

Deep breathing just before bed is one of my favorite remedies for insomnia! It is cheap (free!), can be done anywhere, and takes very little effort or planning. Preferably, do your deep breathing before you lie down, perhaps in a chair, after you have completed all preparations for bed. Close your eyes, relax your body, and breathe in all the way down to your navel. Slowly exhale. Imagine breathing in calm and peace, imagine breathing out stress and anxiety. Maintain your deep breathing and your visualization for at least 5 minutes. Slowly open your eyes. Slip into bed, continuing to think of calm and peace. ZZZZZZZZZZ.

Light, Dark, and Noise

Ever try to sleep with the lights on? Some people can, some people can't. Regardless, most people find that they fall asleep more easily in total darkness. When staying in hotels, I look forward to the *total darkness* provided by the blackout curtains that many hotels use. I sleep SO well that I now have similar curtains at home! Total darkness sends a strong message to our brain that it REALLY is time to sleep. Total darkness also gives the pineal gland a time for rest and restoration, making sleep far more restful.

To increase the darkness for sleep, obtain a *sleep mask*. (You won't always be in the perfect hotel room.) Travel stores carry sleep masks, some airlines give them away on overseas flights, and you also may find them in drugstores. Some people swear by sleep masks containing magnets, such as the sleep mask manufactured by Nikken (a multi-level marketing company based in Japan), finding that use of the mask is calming and greatly enhances sleep.

Does noise keep you awake? When I'm traveling, additional sound keeps me awake. The sounds of a bustling city or of your roommate's snoring that recalls a power saw are not restful! I take charge of my environment by carrying a pair of foam *ear plugs*. They are found in travel stores, drugstores, and hardware stores; they are inexpensive and work extremely well. If lack of sound keeps you awake, consider carrying an iPod, MP3 player, or smart phone with earphones. *Background music* helps many to fall asleep. If you have a smart phone, check out the White Noise App to see if it helps you sleep!

Exercise

Have you ever traveled and just ached from the lack of exercise? Sometimes, your failure to fall asleep is linked to your lack of physical activity. Sitting on a plane for 20 hours, sitting in a conference, attending a workshop, driving in a car all day — these activities may exhaust you but do not provide exercise. Many of us need a *minimum level of exercise* in order to sleep. Taking a long walk, going for a run, swimming, or engaging in your sport on a daily basis may be enough to ensure a good night's sleep. Try to exercise at least two hours before bed because exercise can awaken you! In fact, a walk is a great choice during the afternoon break at conferences — skip the coffee and take a walk!

Baths

How about a *warm bath*? For some people, this is the only thing they need to promote good, quality sleep while on the road. Adding 10 drops of *lavender essential oil* to about a tablespoon of milk or shampoo and stirring this into the bath makes the bath more calming and gives you an aromatic, spa-like experience. (A shower does NOT have the same effect!) Plan on spending at least 10–20 minutes in the bath to gain the full, sleep-inducing effect. Afterwards, place a few drops of lavender essential oil on your pillow, pajamas, or wrist to help you to relax and sleep. Ahhh.

Dehydration

Are you one of those people who falls asleep easily when traveling but then awakens in the middle of the night and has trouble falling back asleep? If this happens only when you travel, you may be dehydrated. Try drinking an additional 16–32 ounces of *water* each day. (But don't drink it all just before bedtime!)

Herbal Remedies

In my opinion, our choices of food, lifestyle, and environment are far more important to the quality of our sleep than herbs that we take as supplements. Still, herbs can be invaluable at promoting good quality sleep. Sometimes, you just need more help. I ALWAYS carry sleep herbs when I travel.

For children, *chamomile* is my top choice for sleep. It is sweet, tasty, settles the stomach, clears anxiety, and can be drunk as a tea. It works for adults, too! *Catnip* has similar effects with a pleasant light mint taste. Many children appreciate sweet tasting glycerine-based tinctures that come in dropper bottles. The brand Herbs for Kids makes a good product. Follow directions on the label. For adults, I recommend alcohol-based tinctures, which are stronger and keep longer than the glycerine. (Yes, chamomile tincture can work for you even if the tea doesn't affect you. The tincture is amazing!)

My personal favorite is *kava kava*. Kava commonly is used to clear anxiety and especially helps those of us who go to bed thinking. Kava has a surprising and unusual taste that many dislike but gladly endure because it works so well. Forget the capsules and the pills — get the tincture! The standard dose is 1–4 droppersful. Oh yes, worried about mixing kava with alcohol? You might have had a few drinks with dinner? The

149

cautions on the bottle about not mixing alcohol and kava pertain to much higher doses of kava, not to the therapeutic dose to help you sleep.

Passion flower, valerian, and hops, used separately or (even better) together provide a strong, sleep inducing combination. Take 1–4 droppersful before bed. This combination is especially helpful for people who are easily excited. In high enough doses, valerian is a sedative. (It is not, by the way, related to the drug Valium.) **Caution: A very small percentage of people are sensitive to valerian and find it wakes them up! If you have never used it, try a small dose before you travel.** (If it wakes you up, use *skullcap* herb instead, 1–4 droppersful before bed.)

Ashwagandha, an Ayurvedic herb, is the herb of choice for people who tend towards exhaustion and insomnia. A client of mine, exhausted by her constant travel to tend to an ailing parent that was compounded by the stresses and strains of her own family, asked for help. She described arriving home utterly exhausted and completely unable to sleep. Deep breathing, meditation, long walks — nothing seemed to help. She tried ashwagandha in powdered form, mixing 1 teaspoon of the powder into almond milk 3 times per day. Within days, she could sleep! Her sleep was deep and restful and she felt much less tired. Ashwagandha can be taken in capsules, in powdered form, or as a tincture, and all work well. One particularly good way to take ashwagandha is 1 teaspoon of the powder in scalded milk with honey. It has a unique taste, somewhat earthy and sweet.

I've got to warn you though. Ashwagandha, taken for more than one month, is an effective aphrodisiac! It really increases sex drive. Importantly, it increases sex drive — both in men and women — while nourishing the body. Michael Tierra, a prominent herbalist and the author of *The Way of Herbs*, describes ashwagandha as the "most potent" aphrodisiac. One physician friend who loved the energy enhancing and calming qualities of this herb abruptly stopped using it after one month — she found the aphrodisiac qualities to be way too strong!

Traditional Chinese Medicine (TCM) differentiates among types of insomnia. Can't sleep because you are constantly thinking, worrying, and reviewing? This is true for many students but also for travelers! TCM views this as a Heart/Spleen disharmony—the herbal combination *Gui Pi Tang* may work wonders for you.

Have trouble falling or staying asleep and feel anxious or agitated? Having palpitations? Feel dry and thirsty? Dealing with menopause? For any of these, the herbal combination *Tian Wang Bu Xin Dan* may help. For best results, plan on taking it 3 times per day. These products are available in Chinese herb shops, oriental markets, and many natural food stores, and online.

Homeopathic Remedies

If you commonly have trouble sleeping, consider seeing a homeopath! In the case of sleep, I have found that constitutional treatment by an experienced homeopath is best and worth the expense. I recommend that you try the remedies listed below if the description fits your pattern; if not, remedies in other sections may work for you.

Try *Cocculus* 30c if you are too tired to sleep, especially if you have been sleep-deprived or are jet-lagged. It helps when you have gone to bed much later than usual and cannot sleep or when you have been awakened and cannot fall back to sleep. (Sounds like overnight flights!)

Try *Gelsemium* 30c if anxiety, perhaps your fear of flying or fear of sleeping in a new place, keeps you awake.

Try *Nux vomica* 30c if your over-indulgence is keeping you awake! It also helps you to adjust to your new time zone. This remedy especially helps easily irritated, cold natured, addictive types. Think of the traveler wrapped in her blanket (while everyone else is comfortable) who works while on vacation. Nux vomica also relieves constipation.

Essential Oils

Lavender essential oil is soothing and relaxing. (See the previous section on Baths.) Two or three drops on a handkerchief placed on your pillow or chest is a great sleep aid. Try it for airline travel.

Flower Essences

Combine *flower essences* to help you sleep. Most combinations are not available in stores but you can make your own! Add 2 drops of each remedy to a 1 ounce dropper bottle, add 1½ teaspoons of brandy, and then fill with purified water. From your remedy bottle, take 4 drops immediately before bed. Repeat as necessary.

Rescue Remedy, an outstanding flower essence combination, can be combined with other flower essences for your particular type of insomnia.

General insomnia formula: Cherry Plum, Impatiens, White Chestnut. Cherry Plum helps you to relax and let go, Impatiens helps with impatience, and White Chestnut helps quell repetitive thoughts, worries, and anxiety.

Excitement insomnia formula: Vervain and Rescue Remedy. Vervain helps when your excitement, enthusiasm, or (even) fanaticism keeps you awake. Think of this after concerts, reunions, and rallies.

Grief insomnia formula: Honeysuckle, Walnut,

Rescue Remedy. Honeysuckle helps when your thoughts dwell in the past. Walnut helps you to let go, to release people and thoughts.

Tough decision insomnia formula: Scleranthus and Rescue Remedy. Scleranthus helps when you cannot decide between options and that keeps you awake. Substitute Cerato for Scleranthus if you question your decision and now cannot sleep.

Worries insomnia formula: White or Red Chestnut and Rescue Remedy. White Chestnut helps when repetitive thoughts or worries keep you awake. Choose Red Chestnut when your thoughts are about other people. White Chestnut and Rescue Remedy comprise a commercially available sleep combination, called *Rescue Sleep*. Purchase this online or at natural foods stores or make your own.

Supplements

Vitamin B_1 and Vitamin B_{12} are great sleep aids. Especially if you are experiencing stress (who isn't!), many of us become deficient in B vitamins. Vitamin B_1 (thiamine) helps you to transform starch into energy, supports adrenal function, and is calming. I recommend that you take a B complex that includes 50 mg of B_1. Suffer from fatigue, anemia, muscle weakness, dizziness, or numbness? Especially if you eat few or no animal products, or if you suffer from gluten sensitivity, you may be deficient in Vitamin B_{12}. Choose a sublingual (dissolved under the tongue) Vitamin B_{12} product, even if your B complex includes B_{12}, and take immediately before bed.

Melatonin, a natural hormone that is available at pharmacies, in natural food stores, and online, is a commonly used sleep aid, especially for when travel has changed your sleep schedule or you are traveling across time zones. Take .5 milligrams (500 mcg) just before

INSOMNIA

going to sleep. Personally, I avoid taking hormones. I recommend that you try the remedies above before taking this one.

Insomnia Summary

Lifestyle suggestions:

- No caffeine after noon
  (coffee, tea, drugs, soda, chocolate).
- Drink more water.
- Breathe.
- Meditate.
- Eat high carbohydrate foods in the evening.
- Eat high tryptophan foods.
- Finish eating early in the evening.
- Drink warm milk before bed.
- Take a warm bath (with lavender essential oil).
- Take 2 hours quiet time before bed.
- Reduce light; use an eye mask.
- Reduce noise; use ear plugs.
- Add white noise (Smart phone White Noise App or soothing background music).

Herbs:

- Chamomile.
- Catnip.
- Kava kava.
- Passion flower, hops, and valerian.
- Ashwagandha.
- Gui Pi Tang (Chinese herbal formula).
- Tian Wang Bu Xin Dan.

Insomnia Summary, continued

INSOMNIA

Homeopathics:

- Cocculus 30c (for insomnia when you are too tired to sleep).
- Gelsemium 30c (for insomnia from fear or dread).
- Nux vomica 30c (for cold natured, constipated, irritable workaholics).

Essential oils:

- Lavender essential oil.

Flower essence formulas:

- **General**: Cherry Plum, Impatiens, White Chestnut.
- **Excitement**: Vervain and Rescue Remedy.
- **Grief**: Honeysuckle, Walnut, Rescue Remedy.
- **Tough Decision**: Cerato or Scleranthus, Rescue Remedy.
- **Worries**: Red Chestnut or White Chestnut, Rescue Remedy.

Supplements:

- Vitamin B_1.
- Vitamin B_{12} (sublingual).
- Melatonin.

JET LAG

Jet lag is the physical and emotional discomfort we experience after rapidly passing through multiple time zones. People may experience headaches, lack of appetite, profound sleepiness, exhaustion, irritability, or disorientation. The effects of jet lag vary greatly from person to person, but the effects are very real. People experience jet lag in different ways and to different degrees.

Jet lag always has fascinated me. It only occurs with travel from east to west or west to east. When traveling across fewer than 12 time zones, traveling east is more likely to produce jet lag than traveling west. All people who travel by air across at least two time zones experience jet lag. Although some may not notice it and others may have debilitating symptoms, everyone "gets" it. It is a function of our time, that today we can move so quickly that our bodies literally are left behind.

Jet lag costs us time and money. For the vacationer, jet lag may ruin a substantial portion of a trip or may result in illness following the trip home. The person traveling for business will be at a competitive disadvantage in any negotiation immediately following rapid travel across time zones.

My first major experience with jet lag occurred after flying to Australia. I thought I knew what to expect. I arrived in Sydney, 13 time zones from my home on the east coast of the United States. No headache, no malaise, no exhaustion. "I don't have jet lag," I said to myself. An hour later, I was walking along the beautiful Sydney Harbor looking at the blue skies and the fabulous skyline. Then, for no apparent reason, I burst into tears. I couldn't stop crying. I looked around — nothing was wrong, everything was fine. But I felt as though I was at the bottom of a dark and dank pit, completely lost and utterly incapable of continuing on my journey.

Finally, I called friends in Canberra, Australia. They asked how my trip had gone, I snuffled on the phone, and my friend Helen exclaimed, "You have jet lag!" She, a seasoned traveler, assured me that it would pass and that I would not always feel this way. She was right. It took about 3 days to pass on its own. YOU can do better!

Jet Lag Reduction Program

The heart of the jet lag reduction program is *rest, rehydration*, and *resetting your inner clock*. Judicious use of caffeine helps. Supplementation also helps. Minimization of jet lag requires advance planning and preparation, but you can do it!

Preparation

Seven days prior to your trip, read this Jet Lag section in its entirety. Decide which homeopathic remedies, herbs, and supplements you will bring and obtain them now. Obtain a travel bag for your remedies.

At least 3 days prior to your trip, *stop drinking coffee and ingesting all other sources of caffeine*. Begin fully hydrating your body with high quality *water*, at least 1 ounce of water daily for every 2 pounds of body weight, or at a minimum, 64 ounces of pure water a day. Take at least 3,000 milligrams of natural *vitamin C* each of those three days. Obtain *Rescue Remedy*, a product for stress available at most health food stores, and begin taking 4 drops at least 3 times (preferably 6 times) per day. (Alternatively, put 4 drops of Rescue Remedy in your water bottle and sip during the day.) *Rest* a minimum of 8 hours per night.

Three days before your trip, *change your exposure to light*. When traveling east, avoid outdoor light for the last 3 hours of daylight, and go to bed earlier than usual. When traveling west, avoid outdoor light for the first 3 hours of daylight.

JET LAG

To assist the pineal gland in resetting your inner clock, some travelers take *a small dose of melatonin,* a natural hormone. Melatonin also will help you sleep. Take 500 mcg just before going to sleep on the plane and just before bedtime after you arrive at your destination.

Prepare a *travel bag* with everything you need for your trip. Leave room for at least 1–2 liters of pure *water* for times when beverage service is not available. (Purchase your water at the airport after you clear security.) Obtain a soft and comfortable *sleep mask* and *ear plugs,* both available at pharmacies and travel stores. Consider bringing noise cancelling headphones. They really work, and the reduced noise helps you sleep and reduces stress from airplane engine noise. At your local health food store, obtain *vitamin C,* preferably a natural C with 1,000 milligrams per dose. (I like traveling with Emergen-C, an excellent and tasty powder that comes in individual packets and dissolves in water.) Pack any herbs that you have used to assist you in falling asleep; good choices include *kava kava,* a *passion flower-hops-valerian* combination, or *chamomile.* Pack single homeopathic remedies, choosing from the list later in this chapter. If you choose to use melatonin, purchase 500 mcg at your local health food store or pharmacy. Pack 3 or more high quality *protein or meal replacement bars.* Pack single portion soft-sided salmon packages and soft-sided meat jerky packages. Pack *candied ginger* to eat if you feel a cold coming on, if you become chilled, if you feel nauseated, or if you begin to feel motion sickness. Pack *nuts and seeds* for snacking. If you will be traveling for three or more night-time hours, pack *socks* for sleeping or extra soft slippers. Be sure to pack your *toothbrush and toothpaste.* Pack your book or magazines. Pack any *medications and copies of their prescriptions*!

Airport security rules in many nations limit the size of liquid and gel containers to 100 milliliters each (about 3.4 ounces), require that they all fit in a 1 quart plastic bag, and recommend you place the bag separately in the inspection bin. If you carry liquid herbs, homeopathic remedies, supplements, or moisturizers, place them in your 1 quart bag. Finish preparing your travel bag at least 3 days prior to your trip.

Departure Day

Remember to bring your travel documents, identification, money, and credit cards.

Place any additional food in your travel bag. Carry your travel bag with you in your carry-on luggage.

Purchase 1–2 liters of water after you clear security and place them in your travel bag.

Board the plane, settle yourself in your seat, and take your homeopathic remedy. Plan to take 1 dose every 4 (waking) hours and upon arrival. Place your travel bag under the seat, NOT in the overhead bin. Breathe. Relax.

As soon as the plane departs, *set your watch* to the current time at your destination. Note the time and begin thinking in terms of the new time. From now on, be disciplined and think only of the destination time. Remember, you are resetting your inner clock, not just your watch. While you are awake, check your watch at least every waking hour, telling yourself the destination time and what you ordinarily do at that time.

After setting your watch, drink 16 ounces of water. This is why you brought water with you. *Drink only bottled water* and do NOT accept ice! You have no idea of the source of the plane's water or the cleanliness of the water storage. When the steward comes, talk him into letting you have a large or multiple small bottles of water to keep at your seat. Drink 8 ounces of water for every hour that you are on the plane. At that rate, a liter lasts 4 hours.

Take 1 gram (1,000 milligrams) of *vitamin C*. Take NO ALCOHOL and NO CAFFEINE. No caffeine means no coffee, no tea, no colas, no Mountain Dew, no Surge, no Jolt!, and no chocolate. (OK, maybe just a little chocolate!) No alcohol means no liquor, no cordials, no beer, and no wine. If you feel bad about missing free drinks on international flights, just tell yourself that both caffeine and alcohol are dehydrating and that dehydration makes jet lag much worse. You can celebrate later! Feel virtuous in your discipline.

Take *demulcent herbs* that moisten from the inside out if you get stuffy when you fly. Take *marshmallow root* or *asparagus root*, either 2 capsules, 1 dropperful of the tincture, or 1 cup of the tea every hour or two. These demulsifying (softening and moistening) herbs soothe the mucus membranes that become irritated by the dry cabin air. The membranes will relax and the stuffiness will disappear. *Spraying your face with water* or a saline solution also will help. Keep drinking your water!

Put on your *noise cancelling headphones*. Noise inside the passenger cabin may average 100 decibels during your flight! This is above safe levels. The noise adds to your stress and studies show that it also can cause fatigue, irritability, loss of appetite, nausea, dizziness, headache, difficulty sleeping, distraction, and poor memory. Those sound like jet lag symptoms! Noise cancelling headphones can reduce noise by 40 decibels, greatly improving your comfort. I use them on all long flights! Purchase them at electronics stores or online. Don't forget the batteries. *Foam earplugs* are a less expensive, easier-to-carry option.

Plan to go to sleep at your regular sleep time according to your watch. This may be very different from the schedule on the plane. As you approach "bedtime" begin winding down. Do as much of your sleep preparation routine as you can. *Take your relaxing herbs* (chamomile, kava kava, or passion flower-valerian-hops) and melatonin, take off your shoes, and put on your slippers. Finally, put in your earplugs if you are not wearing headphones, turn off your seat light, place your seat in its reclining position, put on your sleep mask, and begin slowing and deepening your breathing. The darkness provided by your sleep mask is key to resetting your inner clock. *Believe that you will fall asleep.* Even if you do not immediately fall asleep, continue to rest in this position. Try your best to sleep or rest for at least four hours. (Do not worry that you will insult the stewards or look stupid.)

When you are not sleeping or resting quietly, *get up and walk at least every 1–2 hours*. Developing blood clots is a real danger on long flights. You reduce the likelihood by drinking your water, avoiding caffeine, and getting up and walking. Really! You also reduce leg and foot swelling and relieve your back. It is NOT SAFE to stay seated for hours and hours.

During your flight, *avoid all light until dawn* at your destination. At dawn, feel free to look deeply at light. Watching the sunrise really will help! Drink at least another 16 ounces of water and take 1 gram of vitamin C.

Destination Day

Today, what you eat, drink, and think will make a huge difference in how you fare during the next 24 hours. Look at your watch and consciously tell yourself the destination time. ("I am in Japan, it is 8 a.m., it is time for breakfast.") Remember, you are anchoring yourself in the destination time.

At morning for your destination, drink 1–2 cups of *coffee, tea*, or *hot chocolate*! Go ahead and have some caffeine! Caffeine at this time helps your body to catch up to the new time zone. Also, if you regularly drink caffeine as a morning beverage, drinking it now helps to cement the mindset that this is indeed morning. You will NOT have any caffeine after noon. Absolutely NO caffeine at night! Remember, you still are resetting your inner clock.

When breakfast is served, DO NOT eat sugary pastries. *Try to avoid breads and sweets*; they slow you down. If nothing at breakfast appeals to you, open your travel bag and eat one of your protein bars, a handful of nuts, some salmon, or some jerky. Have another gram of vitamin C, and plan on taking at least 3 grams that day. The vitamin C helps to clear toxins from your system (including all the fumes you inhale on board a jet). Vitamin C also helps bolster the immune system and provides a minor energy boost. After breakfast, have another 16 ounces of water.

After You Land

During the morning, *spend at least 15 minutes outdoors*, preferably with your face in the sunshine. Standing in the shade does not count! Sun on your face, even if obscured by clouds, nourishes the pineal gland and helps reset your inner clock. This is a great time to take a walk, which will relieve some of the stagnation of the long flight.

Before each eating event drink at least 16 ounces of pure water. Assume you still are dehydrated. This is your first day at your destination and you need to continue drinking your water. Many planes fly with only 5 percent humidity! The combination of low humidity and your (likely) lack of sleep will deplete your body fluids, also known as your yin. Drink between a half gallon and a full gallon of water that first day, the second day, and the third day.

Feel free to have a mid-morning snack, lunch, and a mid-afternoon snack but *plan on eating small amounts*. Simply by traveling to another time zone, your digestive system has been stressed and fatigued. Taste rather than gorge. Choose non-sugary foods and be gentle on your system. Avoid heavy sauces. Avoid deep fried foods. Do combine non-starchy vegetables (green leafy vegetables) with protein. *Freely take herbal digestive aids*, such as chamomile and ginger. Avoid starchy carbohydrates, like breads, cake, cookies, rice, and potatoes until dinnertime at your destination time. Why? They make you sleepy and you already are exhausted. Reserve them for when you are winding down.

Feeling tired? *Do NOT go back to sleep!* Going back to sleep would let you slip back to your departure time zone. Don't do it! Walk around, drink water, take deep breaths, read, exercise, see what other people are doing, strike up a conversation. Do ANYTHING to avoid sleep. By the way, this is a great time to have some *ginseng*! Two droppersful of ginseng tincture, one 10 milliliter bottle of ginseng extract, 1–2 tea bags steeped for 5 minutes in hot water, or a teaspoon of the root simmered in three cups of water for an hour (serves 2–3 people) will help recharge your batteries. (If you have high blood pressure, don't take panax ginseng — choose American or Siberian ginseng instead.) A packet of Emergen-C dissolved in 8 ounces of water will lift your energy.

If you absolutely MUST sleep, do so, but limit your sleep to 1–2 hours. Set an alarm or have a friend awaken you.

If possible, *avoid alcohol*. If you must have alcohol, limit your consumption to evening. Try to have as little as possible. Alcohol places great stress on the liver, which regulates many of the body's activities. You are

163

consciously avoiding foods and beverages that depress body functions. On the other hand, alcohol can be relaxing — for people who drink, one drink in the evening may help you to sleep.

Sound like a lot to do? It is worth it. You'll see!

Homeopathic Remedies

It is truly amazing how helpful homeopathic remedies are for jet lag. They are invaluable, reducing the extent and severity of jet lag.

Take homeopathic *Cocculus 30c*. Homeopaths view this as a near specific for jet lag because it addresses so many jet lag issues. Perhaps more importantly, it works! Cocculus is for people who are worse (have symptoms) from traveling, have lost sleep because they stayed up too late or had their sleep interrupted, feel drowsy, feel nauseous, have a stiff or aching back, have a headache, are dehydrated, or just feel tired. It also addresses air sickness and sea sickness. For best results, take 1 pellet the night before you travel, 1 pellet upon taking your seat on the plane, and then 1 pellet every 4 waking hours or as needed during the flight. Take 1 dose when you land, and then take 1 dose as needed during your journey.

Consider Cocculus first for any ailment on your trip! It will address most travel problems. Cocculus even helps days after travel. I met a friend at a conference who admitted that he felt terrible. He had traveled from Japan to the United States 5 days prior to our conference, but felt nauseated, had no appetite, was exhausted, and felt drowsy but could not sleep. A single dose of Cocculus 30c cleared the nausea, restored his appetite, improved his energy, and enabled him to sleep that night. In the morning, he reported his jet lag was gone! He was fine for the rest of the conference.

Consider substituting homeopathic *Nux vomica* 30c if you tend to be cold, irritable, and constipated and love your caffeine or alcohol. Even if you do not fit the Nux vomica characteristics, carry homeopathic Nux vomica for times when you over-indulge, or if Cocculus fails to clear nausea, indigestion, irritability, headache, nasal congestion or discharge, or constipation.

Bring along homeopathic *Arnica 30c*! Have you ever experienced swollen feet after sitting upright for 20 hours in an airplane seat? Ever had trouble getting your shoes back on? Arnica will help! Take 1 pellet as needed. It also is invaluable for times when you stub your toe, overexert yourself carrying your luggage, bruise, or bleed.

I have met many world travelers who "do not believe" in homeopathy, who nevertheless take *No Jet-Lag*. They take it because it works so very well! This homeopathic combination addresses many jet lag symptoms before they arise. Chew 1 tablet of No Jet-Lag upon boarding the plane, 1 tablet every 2–4 waking hours, and 1 tablet after landing. Then, take 1 tablet as needed for fatigue, sleeplessness, nausea, or other travel ailments. This is a good remedy that I have used with great benefit; if I did not have access to Cocculus, I would use this instead. It contains Arnica 30c, Bellis perennis 30c, Chamomilla 30c, Ipecacuanha 30c, and Lycopodium 30c. Some people find it completely eliminates jet lag. Find it in health food or travel stores or purchase it on the Internet. **One caution**: No Jet-Lag contains the sweetener sorbitol. If you are sorbitol sensitive, it can nauseate you.

JET LAG

Herbal Remedies

Try taking *adaptogens*, herbs that assist the body in adapting to change. An herbal combination that will help with jet lag consists of *astragalus*, *schizandra*, and *Siberian ginseng*. People who commonly experience nausea, motion sickness, or other digestive problems could add *ginger*. This combination strongly enhances the immune system, helps to stop what the Chinese call the "leakage of qi" (loss of energy), builds energy, and improves rest times. It is a warming formula that may be too "hot" for people who usually feel hot when everyone else is cold. For hot people, I recommend a combination of *astragalus* and *burdock root*. Single adaptogenic herbs include ashwagandha, astragalus, burdock root, American ginseng, panax ginseng, rhodiola, schizandra, Siberian ginseng, suma, and tienchi ginseng. (Avoid panax ginseng if you have high blood pressure.) Common dosages are 1–4 droppersful or 0.5 to 2.0 milliliters, or 2 capsules, 1–3 times per day.

Jet Lag Summary

7 days before trip:

- Read Jet Lag Section.
- Choose, purchase, and pack homeopathic remedies, herbs, and supplements.

3 days before trip:

- Drink 64 ounces of water per day.
- Take 3,000 milligrams of natural vitamin C each day.
- Take 4 drops of Rescue Remedy at least 3 (preferably 6) times per day.
- No caffeine 3 days prior to trip (you'll have some after you arrive).
- If traveling east, avoid outdoor light for the last 3 hours of daylight.
- If traveling west, avoid outdoor light for the first 3 hours of daylight.
- Pack your travel bag with supplements, sleep mask, and ear plugs or headphones.

Departure day:

- Add 4 drops Rescue Remedy to your water bottle and drink frequently.
- Pack perishable food and snacks in travel bag.
- Pack medications in travel bag.
- Carry travel documents, identification, money, and credit cards.
- Set watch to destination time upon boarding plane.
- Take 1 pellet of homeopathic Cocculus 30c (or 1 tablet of No-Jet-Lag) upon boarding plane, 1 pellet every 4 hours of flight, and 1 pellet upon landing.
- Drink 8 ounces of water for every hour on the plane and at least 64 ounces per day for the first 3 days at your destination.
- Power on and wear noise cancelling headphones.
- No alcohol. No sugar.

JET LAG

Jet Lag Summary, continued

- If you tend to get airsick, your homeopathic remedy likely will prevent it. If you don't take a homeopathic remedy and feel nauseated, take ginger every 15–60 minutes or as needed.
- During the flight, sleep as much as possible, especially during destination sleep times.
- Take sleep herbs or melatonin to help you sleep.
- Eat small amounts.

Arrival day:

- Have caffeine at breakfast time for your destination. No caffeine after noon!
- Eat a no sugar, low carbohydrate breakfast.
- Natural light, outdoors if possible, at destination.
- Walk or other exercise.
- Do not nap at destination.
- Enjoy a small-portion dinner with starchy carbohydrates.
- Go to bed early. Take sleep herbs or melatonin immediately before bed.

Top packable remedies:

- Sleep mask.
- Noise cancelling headphones or ear plugs.
- Socks or soft slippers.
- Vitamin C.
- Ginger.
- Kava kava.
- Siberian ginseng.
- Melatonin
- Homeopathic Cocculus or No Jet-Lag.
- Bottled water (purchased past security checkpoints).
- Meal replacement or protein bars. Nuts and seeds. Meat jerky, salmon pouches.

MISSING MEDICINES

"I'm sure I brought my medication with me. I have my list, I checked it off. I know that it has to be somewhere." Turning to your husband/wife/travel companion, you ask, "Have you seen my meds?" No, you are told, look in your suitcase. Of course, by now, you have turned your suitcase over on the bed, or you have dumped your pack out on the floor of the tent. You have made a mess, and you STILL have no medication.

You begin going through all your pockets. You wonder when you last took your medication. Did you leave it in the last restaurant? By now, you have been feeling foolish for at least the last half hour, and you are beginning to worry. What are you going to do? You NEED that medication. You NEED whatever it is that you left behind.

Well, if you are in the woods, you have the choice of doing without, borrowing from a companion, finding whatever you need in the wild (you remembered to bring your copy of *Peterson's Medicinal Plants*, didn't you?), calling for help on your satellite phone, or turning back. If you are in an urban area, you can tell yourself that things could be worse. You have options!

Planning for Loss of Your Medication, Herbs, and Supplements

No matter how careful you are, you can forget things, bags can be stolen, and accidents can happen. I recommend that all travelers *carry photocopies of their prescriptions* with them, just in case they lose or forget a medication. Be sure that your prescription includes the name and amount of the medication, the name and phone number of the pharmacy, and the name and phone number of the prescribing doctor. You may need to add some of this information yourself.

Pack all medication, herbs, and supplements in your carry-on or hand luggage. Airlines misplace luggage. Trains misplace luggage. Buses misplace luggage. Stuff gets stolen. Keep your medications, herbs, and supplements close to you.

Make a master list of all medications that you take, where you obtain them, and why you take those medications. Do you take a baby aspirin daily to reduce the threat of stroke? Do you take valerian to help you to sleep? Do you carry echinacea in case you feel a cold coming on? What about your daily multi-vitamin? Your vitamin C? Whatever you use, add it to your master list, including where you obtain it and why you take it.

If you take a commercial (prepackaged) herbal combination, note all of the names on the label (many Chinese patent medicines, which have both a marketing name and a traditional name, are available around the world), the manufacturer or preparing herbalist, and when possible, the list of the herbs in the product. When possible, make a photocopy of the packaging. Whatever you use, add it to your master list, including where you obtain it and why you take it.

If you take a personalized herbal formula, list the names of all the herbs in your native language and in Latin. If the herb is Chinese (or any other non-western tradition), try to list the herbs in your language, in the herbalist's language, and in Chinese. Your herbalist can best guide you with this task, and may direct you to a good herbal text.

For pharmaceuticals, go to your local pharmacy and find out the store's policy for refilling and shipping prescriptions. Confirm that the pharmacy can refill your prescriptions on your request and confirm that the pharmacy can ship to you based upon your phone order. If a more current prescription is needed, contact your physician for a renewed prescription and place the renewed prescription with your pharmacy. If your pharmacy does not provide shipping, contact one that does. An increasing number of pharmacies that make their living by shipping can be found on the Internet. Add the pharmacy's email address, phone number, and fax number to your master list.

Different countries have different rules about what medications may be mailed, purchased, or prescribed. Depending upon your circumstances, you may need to see a local physician for prescriptions.

For herbs and supplements, go to your preferred health food store and confirm that the store will ship to you based upon a phone order. Add the health food store's email address, phone number, and fax number to your master list.

Obtain a prepaid phone card. At the time of this writing, large discount warehouse stores provide some of the lowest prices in the United States, and phone companies provide some of the highest! A prepaid card can save you a lot of money — hotels and public phones may charge hundreds of times the rate you would pay on a prepaid card. Obtain an international card for international travel. Check current prices and purchase a card. If you need to reorder your medications, your prepaid phone card will help.

Carry your master list in two places — with you in your pocket, purse, fanny pack, small personal luggage, or with your passport AND someplace else, such as in your luggage or backpack. If you have one, input your list on your iPhone or other mobile device. Be sure to include all prescription and over-the-counter medications, herbs, homeopathics, and supplements. If you know what you lost, you often can replace it. Depending upon where you are traveling, you may be able to replace all you have lost in local pharmacies, stores, and herb shops or by having something shipped. Your list will be invaluable.

Replacing Lost Medication, Herbs, and Supplements

Know that you can replace anything you have lost. (Personally, I start walking around looking for local plants. But that is me!)

Obtain a signed police, airline, or hotel manager's lost, missing, or stolen report detailing the time, date, and loss. If the police, airline, or hotel manager does not ordinarily write such reports, you may write one of your own, signed both by you and the officer or a manager. If no official will sign, try to have someone else, even a travel companion, sign as a witness. You may need this later, especially if you will be replacing prescription drugs. It also may be helpful for insurance purposes.

Review your master list and determine what you need to replace. In metropolitan areas of the United States, you often can obtain everything you need in a large grocery that includes a pharmacy. In many other places, you may need to visit a pharmacy, natural products store, grocery, and herb shop. Phone books, the internet, global positioning devices (GPSs), smart phones, and hotel concierges are helpful for obtaining the names and locations of stores.

Replace prescription medicines FIRST. This often is the most difficult and time-consuming. Ask to see the pharmacist, show her or him your prescription copies, and ask for help. Charm and sincerity go a long way here. Local laws may be very strict — you may be asking a BIG favor of the pharmacist in requesting that she or he fill the prescription. You may need to see a local physician.

Having trouble obtaining replacements? Consider

having things shipped. (See "Planning for Loss of Your Medication, Herbs, and Supplements.") This often is the least costly, least troublesome solution. Many U.S. pharmacies will ship to you, so long as you are located in a U.S. territory or can receive mail through an army, fleet, or diplomatic post office (APO, FPO, DPO). If you are not, consider www.drugstore.com, which is located in the United States and partners with a shipping company that delivers internationally. Some online pharmacies outside the United States will ship product to you almost anywhere in the world. The larger health food stores in my area ship all over the United States and occasionally around the world. Most professional herbalists keep meticulous records of your herbal combinations — some of them will ship directly to you. Know that UPS (United Parcel Service), FedEx (Federal Express), and DHL ship to most places around the globe, often overnight.

MISSING MEDICINES

Missing Medicines Summary

Plan for loss of medications, herbs, and supplements:

- Photocopy all prescriptions.
- Make a master list. What you take, why you take it, Latin or trade name, and phone and fax number of store that will refill or replace item.
- Confirm that stores will refill or replace from a phone call.
- Update prescriptions as needed.
- Obtain a prepaid phone card.
- Carry a hard copy of your master list in 2 places and on your mobile device.
- Carry your medications, herbs, and supplements with you.

Replacing lost medications, herbs, and supplements:

- Know you can replace everything.
- Obtain a signed report describing the loss.
- Review your master list.
- Replace prescription medications first. If you cannot replace items locally, have the items shipped to you.
- Replace all other medications, herbs, and supplements. If you cannot replace items locally, have the items shipped to you.

MOTION Sickness

The day I finished writing this section, I closed my computer and drove to my martial arts class. Our instructor laid out mats and had us perform rolls — over and over again. Although this is an important skill, it is not one that we usually practice, so it was an unaccustomed movement for me. We rolled continuously for around 30 minutes. At the end of class, my stomach hurt and I felt feverish and generally rotten. I mentioned to a classmate that I thought that I was getting sick, and that it felt like flu! She considered a moment and said that maybe the rolling motion made me sick. Motion sickness!

I ran to the local grocery, went to the produce department, and broke off a small piece of ginger. I skinned it with my thumb and gnawed off a piece the size of the nail on my pinky. I chewed it and considered how I felt. No immediate effect. I thought, "Well, I might as well pick up some water." By the time I reached the water, maybe 2 minutes later, I realized things had changed. No stomach ache. No fever. No nausea. Wow, I thought, gone in 2 minutes! Not quite. It started coming back. I chewed a little more, same result. Nausea gone for 5 minutes, nausea returned, chewed more ginger, nausea gone for 5 minutes, chewed more ginger. In all, I probably had 5 or 6 bites. Afterwards, I had dinner. Success!

The ginger, taken in raw form, relieved about 90 percent of my discomfort. Continued small doses proved important to my recovery. The raw ginger, taken in tiny bites, was mild enough to chew. Relief was almost immediate, but total recovery took some time. I did not feel the need to seek an additional remedy and was able to continue my activities. I definitely include ginger on the list of motion sickness remedies.

MOTION SICKNESS

What Is Motion Sickness?

Motion sickness results when you experience a conflict between what you see and what you feel with the delicate mechanisms of your inner ear. It also results when your body cannot adjust to the unaccustomed change in what it perceives as vertical. People commonly experience motion sickness on boats, in cars, on planes, and in computer-generated "virtual reality."

Herbal Remedies

My favorite all-time remedy for motion sickness is *ginger*. Ginger candy. Ginger tea. Ginger tincture. Ginger capsules. If it has real ginger in it, it will work. I highly recommend that people prone to motion sickness carry ginger on all trips. Ginger is widely used as a spice and is commonly viewed as safe and effective.

You can find candied ginger in oriental food markets (the lowest price source), in natural food markets, and in gourmet shops. The candy does not need refrigeration and packs well. Taste it before you go — some ginger is VERY sharp and may not be to your taste.

Ginger tea is available in oriental food markets, natural food stores, and occasionally in grocery stores. You can make your own tea from fresh ginger, which is widely available in produce departments. Grate or slice approximately 1–2 inches of the root into 2 cups of water. Simmer for 20–30 minutes and drink. Personally, I find that the fresh ginger tea works best of all. You also can make the tea from ginger powder, which you can find in the spice department in groceries or in oriental markets. Simmer 1 teaspoon of ginger powder in 2 cups of water for 20–30 minutes.

You can obtain ginger capsules at pharmacies and at natural food and health stores. (These are just powdered ginger — the ground spice — that has been placed in capsules.) Many people who travel on cruise ships bring them along. Some non-cruising travelers bring a few capsules with them for emergencies. Capsules are lightweight and require no water or cooking.

When I travel, I bring a 1 ounce bottle of ginger tincture with me. When I feel distress, I take 1 dropperful of the tincture. Advantages of the tincture include its easy packability and its immediate effect. In alcohol, the herb enters the bloodstream more quickly, so it works very fast. You can add a 1–2 dropperful of ginger tincture to hot water for a quick and easy cup of tea on the road. Yum!

Ginger is SUCH a good remedy that I recommend ALL travelers take it with them. It is good for so many digestive problems, including nausea, gas, fish or other food poisoning, and many different stomach aches. It helps to clear a cold or flu before it takes hold and helps with cold and flu symptoms. It will warm you if you have become overly chilled. Soaking your feet in ginger tea will relieve foot aches from too much walking. Taken internally, it helps to relieve women's menstrual cramps. It is a delicious beverage that is mildly energizing but will not keep you awake. What a pal!

Begin any herbal remedy at least 1 hour before travel. If taking ginger, take some every 15–60 minutes and more frequently when necessary. If you start feeling queasy, take more! Although all forms of ginger are effective, I personally like the convenience and chewing of crystallized ginger.

Other herbal remedies for nausea include *peppermint* and *chamomile*. If you tend towards reflux, skip the peppermint. If you dislike any herbal remedy, choose another!

MOTION SICKNESS

Homeopathic Remedies

Travelers who prefer homeopathic remedies should try *Cocculus* 30c or *Nux vomica* 30c. Place 1 pellet beneath your tongue about one hour prior to travel. Repeat this dose as needed (when symptoms arise) and every 15 minutes if you feel motion sickness. Other great choices include *Tabacum* 30c for people who get nauseated with headache and sometimes dizziness or *Petroleum* 30c for people who get nauseous with dizziness, heartburn, and possible belching. Think of Nux vomica 30c if you have successfully used this remedy in the past or if you are trying to work, have a headache, and are irritable. Use the same dose and frequency listed above. See "Choosing Homeopathic Remedies," page 21.

Flower Essences

Take *Rescue Remedy* for motion sickness, especially if travel makes you nervous. This combination flower essence works amazingly well for nauseated cats, infants, children, or adults! On animals or infants, rub 2–4 drops into the ears or feet. Children and adults can take 4 drops directly beneath the tongue or in a bottle of water to be sipped. For best results, begin taking Rescue Remedy 15 minutes before travel and continue hourly or as needed.

Foods and Supplements

Eat small portions prior to travel and avoid acid foods like orange juice, tomato juice, coffee, and fried foods. Vitamin B_6, 100 mg. per day, helps some people avoid nausea. Alternatively, eat at least one cup of *parsley* or *dark green leafy vegetables* per day. This food remedy helps some people avoid nausea.

Pharmaceutical Remedies

Medical doctors commonly prescribe *Dramamine* (dimenhydrinate) for motion sickness. It has a long history of successful usage but many people do not like the common side effect — sleepiness. Review all contraindications prior to purchase. Dramamine cannot be taken with certain medications and should not be taken by people with glaucoma, enlarged prostate, emphysema, or chronic bronchitis. Do not take with alcohol. If you will be scuba diving, find another remedy because Dramamine can cause inebriation with high pressure. If you choose to take this medication, take it at least 1 hour prior to travel, and then every 4–6 hours.

Ginger, the herb mentioned previously, has performed better in some motion sickness studies than Dramamine. In one of those tests ginger and Dramamine were both given every 4 hours, and ginger was found superior. Ginger would have worked even better if it had been given more frequently!

More recent to the market is *Bonine* (meclizine). Many people prefer it to Dramamine because it has it doesn't make them as sleepy. If you choose to take this medication, take it at least 1 hour prior to travel, and then every 24 hours. Side effects include sleepiness, dry mouth, and possibly blurred vision.

Comparing ginger with Bonine, Bonine is stronger but takes time to work. Ginger, especially crystallized or ginger tincture, works almost instantly. I have met cruise passengers who take a capsule of ginger at lunch on the day that they sail and continue taking it every 2–4 hours. They carry Bonine just in case, and switch to Bonine only in the event of very heavy seas AND if their ginger fails to counteract the nausea.

Other people use a prescription skin patch called *Scopalamine*, which must be applied 6–8 hours prior to travel. Apply the patch in the hairless area behind one ear. If you need assistance with motion sickness for more than 3 days, discard and replace the patch every 3 days, using alternate ears. Wash your hands thoroughly after touching the patch! A derivative of belladonna, Scopalamine may cause sleepiness, dry eyes, dry mouth, and a variety of other side effects. Serious side effects may include extreme fear, confusion, and hallucinations. It is not recommended for use by children. Consult the *Physicians' Desk Reference* (PDR) for further information or speak with your doctor or pharmacist.

Acupressure

You can use acupressure on yourself to eliminate motion sickness — you press and "grind" your thumb against the inside of your opposite wrist. Find the spot by turning the arm so the palm faces up. Place your thumb in the center of the "crease" in the wrist, move your thumb 2 finger widths towards the elbow and press. Feel the hollow spot between the tendons? That's it! Called "Pericardium 6," "P-6," "Inner Gate," or "Neiguan," it is used for many different functions, including treatment of nausea, vomiting, digestive pain, acid reflux, hiccups, and belching. It also helps to sedate PMS emotionality and is generally calming to both men and women. This really works and the effect will be felt within 5–10 seconds!

Natural products manufacturers have seized upon the proven value of this acupressure point and have provided a variety of *wrist bands and wrist straps* that stimulate P-6 for you. Available online, in natural products stores, at some pharmacies, and in on-board cruise ship stores, these typically have a small plastic or magnetic bump that is placed directly over the point. The wrist bands and wrist straps cost $10–20. Both the plastic and magnetic versions have been found to be effective. I recommend that motion sickness sufferers try these products and use them with ginger. They are a MUST for long sailing trips, even for individuals who have not yet suffered from motion sickness. Prolonged rough seas can do in anyone, but you can be prepared.

Other Helpful Hints

When in a *moving car, train, or ship, focus your eyes on the horizon.* This will limit the movement that is disturbing you. If you tend towards motion sickness, avoid reading. Position yourself to minimize motion — on a plane, sit over the wing; in a car, sit in the front seat. When traveling by car, you may want to drive; many people experience less motion sickness when they drive than when they ride as passengers.

Many people are sensitive to the rocking motion on board boats and ships. Strive to *maintain your head in a perfectly vertical position.* When the ship rolls to the right, compensate by shifting to the left. Fresh air and well-ventilated spaces help many people. Move away and stay away from big smells such as fish, diesel fumes, chemicals, or cooking odors.

MOTION SICKNESS

MOTION SICKNESS

Motion Sickness Summary

Food recommendations:
- Eat lightly.
- Avoid orange juice, tomato juice, coffee, and fried foods.

Herbal remedies:
- Ginger.

Homeopathic remedies:
- Cocculus 30c.
- Nux vomica 30c.
- Tabacum 30c.
- Petroleum 30c.

Flower essences:
- Rescue Remedy.

Supplements:
- Vitamin B_6.

Pharmaceutical remedies:
- Dramamine or Bonine or Scopalamine patch.

Acupressure:
- Press P-6 on both wrists.

Other helpful hints:
- Don't read.
- Gaze at the horizon.
- Hold head vertically.

Top packable remedies:
- Ginger in all forms.
- Cocculus 30c.
- Motion sickness wrist straps.

PARASITES

I had just come back from a great trip to Arizona and was sitting with my herbal study group. I was excited and ready to describe my trip. I felt flushed — was it the excitement? I found myself sweating — had it been that hard to bring my books into our study room? My abdomen hurt — was I starting my menses early with the stress of travel? I had a slight headache — dehydration from the plane? It was becoming increasingly hard to focus. My abdomen felt hot and the pain increased. I felt nauseated. I had diarrhea. Was it appendicitis? I was having trouble focusing. My colleagues, all medically trained, asked if I was OK. Oh, sure, I said, wondering how I would drive myself home. Wisely, my group insisted that a medical doctor check me for possible appendicitis.

Thirty minutes later, the doctor manually checked my appendix — no problem. She looked at me: still sweating, heart racing, nauseated, and in pain. She had one question for me, had I been traveling? Yes, but it was all within the United States. No camping. No lake or river water. She laughed and said that if someone with my symptoms answered yes to travel, ANYWHERE, that she treated the person for parasites. Why, I asked? She shrugged her shoulders, said that testing took too long, and that treatment for parasites usually cleared the problem.

My doctor wrote out a prescription for a strong anti-parasite drug, Flagyl, which has common side effects of nausea, loss of appetite, and low energy. She told me that it was a "rough" but effective medicine and said that I had 48 hours to clear the symptoms on my own before I needed to fill the prescription. I began taking anti-parasite herbs, a combination of *black walnut hull*, *cascara sagrada*, *clove*, and *wormwood* every 20 minutes, and my symptoms shifted within an hour.

183

Amazing! My condition changed so quickly that I wondered what really had happened. And I wondered how we get parasites and how many of us have them.

Who Has Parasites?

First of all, *everyone gets and has parasites*. Everyone. This includes rich people and poor people and people in rural, suburban, and metropolitan areas. People with pets, and people without them. Outdoor types and office workers. One naturopathic doctor said that to be human means having parasites.

You believe you are different? You bathe every day, drink only bottled water, and eat only the cleanest food? Well, I suggest that you look at your skin under a 200x to 500x powered microscope. Those creatures you see moving on your skin may look as though they are from another planet. They are on you, they live on and in you, and they are called parasites. No amount of scrubbing will totally eliminate them. We probably need them! (Well, some of them.)

We get parasites from the air that we breathe, the surfaces that we touch, the water that we drink, and the food that we eat. Parasites are easily spread through human and animal contact, through feces, through raw foods, through sewage, through dirt, and by insects. Parasites are spread through simple handshakes, children's play, and sex. Really, the list goes on and on.

Parasites are living creatures that live on or in us, at our expense. They vary in size from the tiniest microorganisms visible only under high powered microscopes to worms measured in feet or meters. Most of the time, we live in balance with our parasites. Travel may introduce us to unaccustomed parasites that precipitate a major response in our bodies, making us ill.

Symptoms of parasite infestation may include dysentery, vomiting, profuse sweating, and many other uncomfortable symptoms. Minor symptoms include anal or ear itching, diarrhea, cravings for unusual foods (such as charcoal, dirt, clay, and raw rice), and major changes in appetite. Other symptoms include digestive disorders, many skin conditions, mental fog, memory problems, sleep problems, and various aches and pains.

Most travelers don't have time for testing. As my doctor suggested, *when you suspect parasites, treat for parasites.* My personal rule of thumb — assume parasites if the person has ear, nose, or anal itching. When traveling in areas of known contamination, assume you will come in contact with parasites (yes, even at five-star hotels!) and respond accordingly. If non-sterile water touches your lips or eyes in those areas — you have parasites. Take immediate action.

Reducing the Likelihood of Parasite Infestation

You can reduce the likelihood of parasite infestation by following a few simple rules.

Wash your hands frequently and thoroughly with soap, especially following personal elimination, following raw food preparation, and following personal contact with other people. Studies have shown that thorough washing with soap and water is the best method for reducing germs. Ever been in a bathroom and there was no soap? Carry your own small bar of soap — it is portable and lightweight.

No water or soap? *Always carry hand sanitizer.* Made of alcohol in a jelled form, hand sanitizer kills parasites as well as bacteria and viruses. The 1 ounce squeeze bottles fit easily in your purse, pack, or pocket. Carry up to the 3.4 ounce (100 ml) size on planes. I find it invaluable on the road for fast bathroom breaks. Soap and water continue to be your first choice though; the alcohol in hand sanitizers can dry out your skin and long-term use kills too much beneficial bacteria.

185

PARASITES

Make Your Own Hand Sanitizer

Store-bought hand sanitizer is inexpensive, but you can control the quality of ingredients when you make your own.

2/3 cup (160 ml) pure grain alcohol or 91% isopropyl alcohol

1/3 cup (80 ml) aloe vera gel (store-bought or scraped from inside the aloe plant leaf)

8–10 drops lavender or tea tree essential oil

Stir thoroughly and store in bottles or salve jars. Using a higher percentage of aloe will reduce the strength but will increase the solidity. Label and use.

Avoid touching your face and especially avoid contact between your hands and your face. Assume that whatever is on your hands will end up in your mouth so keep your hands away!

Taking grapefruit seed extract (GSE) internally on every day of your trip and for at least 3 days following your trip greatly reduces the risk of parasite infestation. This is a fabulous remedy! I take it and it works (though the extract tastes terrible!). Follow the directions on the label. This is available in natural food stores, online, and in some pharmacies. It comes in 1 to 4 ounce dropper bottles, capsules, and tablets.

Pepto-Bismol (bismuth subsalicylate) tablets can be taken to avoid traveler's diarrhea. The manufacturer states that the product is anti-bacterial; it's widely available at food markets and pharmacies. The dose is 2 tablets 4 times per day on every day of your trip and for at least 3 days following your trip. Be prepared for a black tongue and black stool from this product. Medical doctors recommend that you limit use to 3 weeks. You also can take Pepto-Bismol to treat diarrhea. I don't take this product, but I would if I had nothing else. Caution: Do not take this product with aspirin; it shares ingredients with aspirin and taking both can lead to salicylic acid overdose. Check first with your doctor if you take blood thinners or if you have gout. Do not give to children under the age of 12. Do not give to children with flu or chicken pox — their use of salicylate-like compounds may increase the risk of Reye's Syndrome. Some people are allergic to this medicine, and some experience severe side effects. Bring the package insert with you and read it.

How well do grapefruit seed extract and Pepto-Bismol work? Trekking groups I've spoken with use either remedy and report little or no traveler's diarrhea! That is amazing when you consider that 40–60 percent of travelers visiting "high risk" developing countries contract traveler's diarrhea!

Don't eat raw or undercooked meat or fish. Many microorganisms live in raw meat, poultry, and fish. Many parasites survive searing, flash frying, or other quick-cooking methods that leave the meat succulent, juicy, and rare. Most of them are killed by high heat or extended cooking. You don't need to order your meat burnt, but I would order at least medium to avoid parasites.

Do not eat sushi or sashimi. Come on, you say, I've eaten sushi for years. Me, too. But it only takes one time with parasites to make you swear off sushi for a long, long time. I LOVE sushi. Still, eating raw fish is a bit like playing Russian roulette. Eventually the bullet will be in the chamber. So I no longer have sushi every week. Oh, you say you only have the cooked or vegetable sushi? Sorry, you are still at risk. The knife and the cutting board that touches the raw fish also touches YOUR California roll!

Do not eat raw shellfish.

In areas known for water contamination, you need

187

to be especially careful to *avoid local water*. In water, parasites can survive simple chlorination. Drink only bottled, well purified, or recently boiled water (boiled for at least 1 minute). Close your mouth when you shower and when you swim. Do not use ice cubes. Do not use ice cubes in the hotel. *Do not use ice cubes* on the airline that is coming from or going to an area with water contamination—moving water to a plane does NOT eliminate the parasites. Travelers in Nepal were stricken with giardia—a particularly nasty single cell parasite—after they drank milk. The milk had been "thinned" with the local water — a common practice!

In areas with known water contamination, *eat no raw salad* — it would have been cleaned with contaminated water. *Eat cooked vegetables and cooked fruit*. If you eat raw fruit, only eat fruit that you peel yourself. If you must have raw vegetables or fruit, clean them thoroughly in a combination of bottled water and grapefruit seed extract.

Brush your teeth with bottled water. Many travelers peel their fruit, eat no raw food, boil their water, and then get sick from using tap water for tooth brushing! If you have no purified water, use wine or a soft drink.

Herbal Remedies for Parasites

Parasites have plagued humans for thousands and thousands of years, and people have found numerous botanical remedies. You can find herbal and food remedies in groceries, natural food stores, gardens, fields, and herb shops. Many are easy to use and extremely effective. Many work as well or better than many of the high-priced pharmaceutical drugs; many anti-parasite drugs ALSO work extremely well. In some situations, drugs are the best choice.

Most commercial herbal preparations for parasites contain a combination of herbs. Several of the herbs may kill parasites, another may reduce the cramping that may occur with parasite die-off, another may help to move them out through the colon. Herbs for parasites include the following:

Garlic bulb	*Cat's claw bark*
Goldenseal root	*Clove bud*
Oregon grape root	*Mugwort (Artemisia vulgaris)*
Ailanthus bark and root bark	*Pau d'arco bark*
Ash tree bark	*Quassia bark*
Barberry root	*Rhubarb (Da huang)*
Betel nut	*Thyme*
Black walnut hull	*Wormwood (Artemisia absinthium)*

Although no single herb (that I am aware of) will kill all parasites, I have seen great success with the combination of *wormwood, black walnut hull, cascara sagrada,* and *clove.* That is the combination I used! (See the beginning of this chapter.) Quassia bark or chaparro amargosa, a desert plant also known as *Castela emoryi,* are other great choices, especially if giardia is suspected.

To treat parasites, I would take a dose of the herbal combination every 20 minutes until symptoms shift, for a total of at least 6 times during the first 24 hours. Then, take 3 doses daily for the next 7 days. It is important to rest from the herbs for 7 days to allow any eggs to hatch. Then, resume the herbs for 7 more days. If symptoms do not shift or only partially improve, increase the frequency. If 6 weeks on this treatment do not eliminate symptoms, change your herbs and consider expanding your anti-parasite strategy.

Anti-parasite herbs tend to be exceedingly bitter,

PARASITES

and most people prefer tinctures or capsules. I recommend 1–2 droppersful of the tincture as a standard dose or 1–2 capsules, 3 times per day. If the combination contains a laxative, it will send you to the bathroom with pretty loose stool. Keep drinking water and persevere.

Foods for Eliminating Parasites

Pumpkin seeds will reduce infestation. Available in grocery stores, natural food stores, and sometimes packaged as a snack food, eating at least 1/4 cup of pumpkin seeds 2 times per day will reduce infestation. Worms don't like the taste of pumpkin seeds! While they are NOT a cure, they are useful in addition to other remedies. Choose raw seeds if possible—they may be more effective than roasted seeds.

Eating raw brown or white rice for breakfast is a traditional Tibetan and macrobiotic preventative and remedy for infestation. Carefully chew a quarter cup (one handful) of raw rice before eating any other food. Chew as thoroughly as possible. Preferably, wait at least 3 hours before taking any additional food. Eat raw rice in the morning for 10 days, rest 5–7 days, and repeat for an additional 10 days. On days that you eat raw rice, an *herbal anti-parasite tea* is especially helpful. Good choices include *mugwort* (artemesia vulgaris) or *fennel*. For severe infestation, fast on raw rice for 10 days and take anti-parasitic herbs.

Eat raw papaya fruit. Papaya purportedly makes the intestines too slippery for parasites! Whatever the reason, papaya reduces parasites and is tasty. Eat a 1 inch slice of fruit, 1–2 times per day.

Camping Supplies

Use a water filtration system or water purifier. A friend who travels extensively always carries a lightweight water purifier, and he stays healthy when everyone else gets sick! I recommend the *SteriPEN*, available at camping stores. It uses UV light to deactivate a wide range of pathogens, including treatment resistant *Cryptosporidium* bacteria, other bacteria, and viruses. It does not change the taste of the water, unlike many chemical cleansers. It is lightweight and easy to use. I have known people who did not purchase it because it just seemed too good to be true. It is not just for camping; some people use it in hotel rooms so they can drink the tap water. Carry extra batteries! This unit is useless without them.

Consider a filtration system, which pairs a fine water filter with chemical (chlorine) water purification. One excellent system is the *MSR Sweetwater*. It does NOT require batteries but it does require that you hand pump your water, which can get tiring. The filter alone eliminates bacteria and many parasites, and the chemical deactivates viruses.

REI, a co-op that specializes in camping and travel supplies, carries an excellent selection of water filtration and purification devices. Shop online or check out one of their stores.

PARASITES

Parasites Summary

Avoid parasites:

- Wash hands frequently. Soap and water.
- Hand sanitizer.
- Avoid touching your face.
- Take grapefruit seed extract or Pepto-Bismol tablets daily.
- Don't eat raw or undercooked meat, fish, or shellfish.
- Eat cooked vegetables — no raw salad!
- Eat only cooked fruit or fruit you peel yourself.

If water contamination is suspected:

- Drink only bottled, purified, or boiled water. Chlorine is NOT enough!
- Don't use ice. Don't use ice. Don't use ice.
- Brush your teeth with bottled water.
- Close your mouth in the shower and when swimming.
- Beware of beverages diluted with water.

Herbal remedies for parasites:

- Black walnut, clove, and wormwood (*Artemesia absinthium*), among others.

Foods for eliminating parasites:

- Pumpkin seeds.
- Raw rice.
- Papaya fruit.

Drugs for eliminating parasites:

- Flagyl, among others.

Camping:

- Water purification devices: SteriPEN, MSR Sweetwater.

STIFFNESS

In my thirties, I was privileged to fence for the Atlanta Fencers Club (AFC). Fencing is a sport that involves 5–10 minute bouts of intense activity followed by sedentary periods while one waits for the next bout. Between the beginning of competition at 8 a.m. and the end of competition at 8 p.m. (or even past midnight!) a fencer might fence 30 bouts.

I remember one year when AFC competed at the Carolina Open, a 2-day event featuring the strongest and largest field of fencers in the Southeast. We jammed 5 of us plus all our gear into a compact car and drove 7 hours straight through to Chapel Hill, the home of the University of North Carolina. Safe at our destination, we unfolded and shook ourselves, trying to shake off our stiffness. We ate dinner, planning for the days ahead. On day one we would give our best for our team; on the second day we would compete in individual competition. Later, we would spend hours in the car driving home.

Oh, did we get stiff! Stiffness occurs when we spend too long a period in a single position. It has happened to us all. You sit in one position for hours on end. Four or 8 or maybe even 12 hours pass. You try to stand and your body seems permanently locked into position. Your joints seem stuck.

Stiffness also occurs when we do too much. Athletes become stiff when they do more than their accustomed training. They compete, rest, and stiffen up.

Travelers experience the double whammy of stiffness suffering: They spend too long in a single position and then over-exert. Think of the times that you have walked and run for planes and trains while dragging heavy bags. Then, think of all the times you have sat in a car, on a bus, in a train, or on a plane, immobile for hours at a time after all that exertion, only to arrive at your destination and over-exert yourself again.

That time at the Carolina Open I was wide open for stiffness from both over-exertion (from competing) and under-activity (from sitting in the car and between bouts). On Saturday, AFC fenced team after team: Each of us fenced four bouts per team. Looking around the stadium, we saw what seemed to be innumerable teams we had not yet fenced but would fence before the day ended. We fenced past midnight for a total of 16 hours of stop-and-go activity. Exhausted, we ate and fell into our beds.

The next morning, the alarm rang at 6 a.m. Four of us were in the room. All awakened at the alarm. None of us moved. I tried to move and could not! It seemed as though my joints had frozen. The alarm continued to ring. Someone called out, "Isn't anyone going to shut that thing off?" Apparently not. The alarm stopped on its own. We lay there, no one moving. Someone asked, "Aren't we fencing today?"

I did not know if I could fence. I did not know if I could get out of bed.

Eventually, we rose, one at a time, to the call of nature.

We dressed for day 2.

We began the competition, keeping silent about our stiffness. I felt a bit embarrassed about feeling so stiff. "Getting old?" I wondered. I didn't want to show weakness, so I told no one.

Despite my stiffness I felt confident: I was highly seeded in the event and my first-round bouts were to be with less experienced fencers. I would need to win only 3 of the next 5 bouts to advance to the second round. I began my pre-competition warm-ups. Movement was difficult, and I decided that I would warm up during, instead of before, the first round.

In my first bout I marveled at my sluggishness and watched in amazement as a rank beginner blanked me, 0-5. That's OK, I thought, I can drop one. I tried stretching before the next bout, running in place, and jumping up and down. For the second bout, I turned up the intensity level. I tried to be fast, I tried to be devious, I tried to be clever. I kept fighting my body — and I lost. Two down, 3 to go.

Clearly, warming up during competition was not enough.

I had about 20 minutes before my next bout. I began jogging around the perimeter of the stadium, moving from a jog to a run as soon as my body allowed. When would this clear? It seemed as though lactic acid ran through my veins, and I felt as though I were underwater. Every joint was stiff. All of my muscles ached. After about 15 minutes the stiffness and the aches began to ease. I ran until my next bout was called. Bout number 3. I needed to win.

With the warmth and the movement from my run, I felt looser, more flexible, and less tight. I focused on my opponent and won my bout! Now it was time to prepare for bout number 4. Typically, I would sit to conserve my energy while I mentally prepared. Not this time! There was no sense in conserving my energy if I were going to lose. I took off on another jog around the stadium and returned for my next bout. Sure, I was getting tired, but the stiffness was leaving. I won the next two bouts, easily. I began to feel like myself again.

[Epilogue: All of us made it to the semi-finals or the finals. I squeaked into the finals and came home with a medal, aching, exhausted, and very happy.]

What Causes Stiffness?

Western medicine tells us that over-exertion stiffness occurs when lactic acid accumulates in our tissues. Chinese medicine tells us that whole-body stiffness, either from over- or under-exertion, results from the accumulation of excess "wind-dampness." Athletes commonly explain mid-performance stiffness by saying they sat too long and got cold. Seniors struggle to stand and say that they sat still for too long. The West, the East, athletes, and seniors all speak of stiffness as resulting from a lack of movement. Let's call it stagnation.

Avoiding Stiffness

Folk wisdom reminds us that a moving hinge never rusts. Stagnation is what allows rust (or lactic acid) to accumulate. *So keep moving!* Coaches recommend that athletes cool down and stretch following intense activity. That is great advice! Coaches recognize that intense activity results in our producing lactic acid and that moderate activity clears lactic acid. After running or fast walking to the plane, train, or bus, most of us plop down into the nearest chair. The result of our intense activity is lactic acid, which stagnates when we plop down. Don't plop! Instead, I recommend that you keep moving. *Walk. Stretch. Do simple calisthenics.*

"Keep moving!" also applies to under-exertion problems of plane, train, bus, and car travel. Try to get up and *walk or gently exercise every one or two hours.* Yes, even when driving, you may wish to pull in to a rest area or a town. Five minutes of walking and stretching every hour will lengthen a car trip slightly but will greatly reduce or eliminate stiffness.

So you say that you are confined to your airline seat? There's turbulence or the person in the aisle seat is sleeping and walking around is impossible? You still can move and exercise many of your joints. Done systematically, you can reduce or even eliminate stiffness from extended sitting. These exercises also could be done at your desk or at a seated event such as a concert or lecture when you feel yourself becoming stiff.

Seated Flex and Rotate Exercises to Combat Stiffness and Increase Flexibility

Flex and rotate all of your joints at least 10 times each. Begin with your toes and work your way up the body.

Toes. Sit back in your seat. Flex, squeeze, and wiggle your toes. Rotate them clockwise, then counterclockwise. Feel awkward? No worries, this will improve with time!

Ankles. Sit back in your seat. Lift your feet off the floor by extending your legs slightly. Flex your ankles by pointing your feet down and away from your body and then reverse the flex by pulling your feet up and towards your body. Rotate your feet clockwise and then counter-clockwise.

Knees. Sit back in your seat. Extend your legs by straightening them, then flex them by bending your legs at the knees. Rotate your lower legs clockwise, then counter-clockwise.

Hips. Sit forward in your seat so that your back no longer touches the back of the seat. Flex your hips by moving them as far as you can to the right, the left, the front and the back. (You CAN do this sitting!) If you can stand, place your feet together and circle your waist and hips clockwise and counter-clockwise. Spread your feet shoulder width apart and circle your waist and hips clockwise and counter-clockwise.

Upper and Middle Back. Sit forward in your seat. Flex your spine by slowly and gently twisting your upper torso to the right and then to the left. Next, imagine that a flexible rubber hose stands up straight

STIFFNESS

and in the center of your body. Rotate your upper body so that it moves clockwise around the hose, and then counter-clockwise. During the rotations your back will briefly touch the back of the seat, then your left side will move slightly to the left, then your chest and abdomen will move forward carrying you away from the back of the seat, then your right side will move slightly to the right. This will feel GREAT.

Shoulders. Sit forward in your seat. Lift your shoulders up towards your ears as high as they will go and then drop them down towards your hips. Now, imagine you are a weight lifter and rotate your shoulders forward while your elbows come forward and then rotate your shoulders back behind you so that your elbows touch the back of the seat and your chest comes forward. Ahh. Next, perform "windshield washer arms." Bring your right arm in front of you with a bent elbow, vertical forearm and open palm facing to the left. Pivoting around your right elbow, press your right hand down towards your left hip and return your hand to an upright position. Do this on both the right and left sides.

Neck. Perform all neck exercises slowly and gently! Sit forward in your seat. Drop your chin towards your chest, relax and feel the stretch in your upper back. Slowly straighten your neck and move your head back as far as it will comfortably go. Relax and jut your jaw towards the ceiling. Gently, slowly, repeat. Next, turn your head to the right as far as it comfortably will go. Gently return to center and repeat to the left side. Look as far to the left as you can. What about the rotations? Some people experience difficulties with neck rotations, so I have not included them. If they are part of your regular exercise program, by all means, do them!

Elbows. Sit forward or back in your seat. Place your elbows on your hips and palms on your thighs. Pivoting at the elbow, raise your forearms off your thighs with your palms facing out, and gently return your forearms to your thighs. Next, keep your elbows on your hips and raise your forearms so that they are halfway between your legs and chest. Pivoting on your elbows, make circles in the air with your forearms. Reverse the circles.

Wrists. Place your elbows on your hips and raise your forearms halfway between thigh and chest. Holding your forearms steady, make circles in the air with your hands. Reverse the circles.

Hands. Place your elbows on your hips. Raise your forearms halfway between thigh and chest, with palms facing each other. Holding your forearms steady, make tight fists and hold for a count of 5, then open your hands as wide as you can and hold for a count of 5.

Treating Stiffness

Taking a long, easy *walk* at the end of the day will help keep the kinks out.

My personal favorite is to take a long *hot bath in Epsom salts*. I recommend that you add at least 1 cup of Epsom salts to a tub of water. Stir the salts into the bath water to dissolve them and plan on soaking at least 10–15 minutes. This can be a life saver. If you wish to add essential oils to the bath, 10 drops of *lavender essential oil* is an excellent choice.

If you prefer showers, you might *try a contrast shower*. Stand under hot water, then switch to the coldest water you can stand, then switch to hot water. I recommend 3 to 5 full cycles. I did this following an intense 12-hour test for my black belt. It works!

An Eastern European coach taught me a sure-fire remedy for use when the next day's performance is critical. It is a harsh remedy, but I include it here because it is THE BEST remedy that I have used for severe over-exertion stiffness. It works better if you have a separate bathtub and shower. Fill the tub with cold water and add a large bag of ice. Get into the tub and stay there at least 1–2 minutes. (He said 5 minutes.) Get out and stand in a hot shower until you have warmed yourself. If you don't have a separate shower, roughly towel yourself, warming yourself with the friction. The coach said to repeat this process 2 more times. (I did not, and it still worked.) Do you need to do an ice bath? Only if contrast showers don't clear your stiffness and you MUST be at your peak the next day. I find it worth knowing.

Massage works! Massage, using deep and long strokes especially, helps to move lactic acid out and helps to relieve stagnation. Imagine that you accumulate puddles of lactic acid that cause stiffness and achiness and imagine that your kneading and stroking of the muscles helps to disperse those puddles. That is pretty close to what happens. Although having your own personal massage therapist certainly helps, you can gain many benefits from self-massage. I prefer to place most of my attention on the large muscles, such as the quadriceps muscles on the top of the thigh. Doing this in the hot Epsom salts bath makes it more beneficial.

Drink water. Drink 1 quart (32 ounces) or 1 liter (about 33 ounces) of water (not beer!) within a 5-minute period. This signals the body to begin flushing itself and will send you repeatedly to urinate. Interestingly, you may urinate more than the amount that you drank! Continue drinking at least 8 ounces (1 cup) per hour. Drinking water in this manner will flush your system of accumulated lactic acid and toxins and will restore the water balance in your body.

You might want to try *apple cider vinegar*! Vinegar has an alkalizing effect on the body and helps to counteract the build-up of lactic acid. Try 1 tablespoon in a large glass of water. I like vinegar water just the way it is, but many people prefer to add a teaspoon of honey. Either way, vinegar will help you to avoid stiffness. Take it at the beginning of a travel or a high activity day and again at day's end. This works for both over- and under-exertion stiffness.

Homeopathic Remedies

If only I had known about homeopathic *Rhus tox-icodendrun* when I was competing in fencing. A remedy made from highly diluted and potentized poison oak, homeopathic Rhus tox is my go-to remedy for stiffness that is better with motion and worse with rest. Rhus tox is perfect for stiffness that results from over-exertion, especially when that stiffness eases with motion. This is a great remedy for seniors, athletes, and all travelers! Think of Rhus on your next trans-Atlantic or trans-Pacific flight, when stiffness from prolonged sitting hits. This is quite different from pain that is better if you hold still and worse if you move it; consider homeopathic *Bryonia* in that situation.

If your stiffness keeps you awake or if you just cannot get comfortable, consider homeopathic *Arnica*. Homeopathic Arnica will help with stiffness accompanied by bruising but also is useful for swelling from prolonged sitting, for bleeding, and for many types of trauma. If Arnica does not seem to help, especially if you sat for hours on end, if you endured extensive bumpy rides (off-road travel), or if your bruising occurred at a deep level, try homeopathic *Bellis perennis*. Although Arnica will work for almost everyone, Bellis can restore areas that Arnica cannot reach.

If I needed Rhus tox, Bryonia, or Bellis and did not have them, I would try Arnica. When I travel, it always is in my pocket. I take it immediately when banged or bruised.

STIFFNESS

Homeopathic Rhus, Bryonia, Bellis, and Arnica are available in natural foods stores, at pharmacies in some countries, and online. I recommend the lower potencies (6c to 30c) for dealing with stiffness. Take 1 pellet of the indicated remedy to assist with stiffness and repeat as needed. Take 1 pellet before bed if you have difficulty with sleeping resulting from stiffness or if you have difficulty moving in the morning from stiffness. Take 1 pellet prior to travel or prior to engaging in physical activity if you commonly experience stiffness. Arnica also will help with recovery from aches and pains, bumps, and bruises.

With homeopathic Rhus tox, Bryonia, Bellis, or Arnica, be prepared for very rapid and sometimes dramatic results. See "Choosing Homeopathic Remedies," page 21, for more information.

Herbal Remedies

An excellent tincture combination that is phenomenal for backaches and stiffness is *Back Support* from Rainforest Remedies — 1 dropperful 3 times per day. Find it online or in select health food stores.

Planetary Herbals has a formula that works well for stiffness. *Flex-Ability* is based on the Chinese formula Shujin San and is available online and in select health food stores. Take 2 tablets 2–3 times per day.

For whole body stiffness that is due to cold (from long periods of sitting, especially in cold places), try multiple doses of *ginger*. Ginger tea, ginger tincture, ginger candy, ginger capsules — all will work. *Cayenne pepper* capsules also will warm and stimulate — take 2 capsules 1–3 times per day. Cayenne pads, salves, or oils effectively warm the skin and can relieve local pain — but do NOT apply to sensitive tissues!

The Ayurvedic medical tradition suggests taking *turmeric* for stiffness — the recommended daily dose is 2 tablespoons. This may be taken daily in water or (more traditionally) in ½ cup of milk. You can find turmeric in kitchens and grocery stores; it's the same as the culinary spice in many curry dishes.

Umeboshi plum neutralizes lactic acid. Take ½ teaspoon of umeboshi plum or paste 1–3 times per day. This food remedy consists of a type of very sour plum that has been preserved in salt. Find it in your health food store, in oriental markets, or online.

Magnetic Therapy

You can use magnetic therapy to reduce or eliminate stiffness. A *therapeutic magnet*, applied directly to the site of pain, reduces pain in many people. If the pain increases, flip the magnet over. Most people secure the magnet in place with tape or a Band-aid. An individual therapeutic magnet will cost between $5 and $50. For whole body stiffness, a magnetic seat pad, mattress pad, or travel pad works very well for many people. The $100–400 price tag is WELL worth it. Smaller magnets are available in drug and health food stores. Magnetic pads are available on the Internet and through multi-level marketing. Some multi-level sellers will allow you to borrow a pad for the night so you can test the pad for yourself. Nikken, a multi-level company, sells excellent magnetic products.

Over-the-Counter Remedies

You say that showers, baths, herbs, and magnets are unavailable and you just want a drug? Sometimes you've got to do what you've got to do. Although these drugs will not eliminate the cause of the stiffness, they will relieve your discomfort. Most over-the-counter analgesic or anti-inflammatory drugs will help: *aspirin*, *ibuprofen* (Advil or Motrin), and *acetaminophen* (Tylenol). Follow package instructions.

STIFFNESS

Stiffness Summary

Causes:
- Lactic acid.
- Chinese: Wind-damp invasion.
- To much or too little exercise.
- Prolonged sitting.

Avoiding stiffness:
- Keep moving. Walk and stretch. Flex and rotate all joints.
- When traveling, walk or exercise every 1–2 hours.

Treating stiffness:
- Walk.
- Epsom salts bath.
- Contrast (hot and cold) shower.
- Ice bath followed by warm shower.
- Massage.
- Drink 1 quart (1 liter) of water within 5 minutes.
- Drink 1 tablespoon of apple cider vinegar.
- Magnets.

Homeopathic remedies:
- Rhus toxicodendrun.
- Arnica montana.
- Bellis perennis.
- Bryonia.

Herbal remedies:
- Back Support (Rainforest Remedies).
- Flex-Ability (Planetary Herbals).
- Ginger.
- Cayenne pepper.
- Turmeric.

MAKING A TRAVEL KIT

As a child, first aid kits fascinated me. I've always liked the idea of being prepared. My father loved to fish, and he would take me with him to the local sporting goods store. I would run to the first aid kits and try to act like an adult shopper as I carefully opened each kit and considered the contents. Some had nothing more than Band-aids, while others had smelling salts, aspirin, and special suction devices for snake bite. Really! The people who manufactured these kits seemed to think that the only things that happened to people were that they would cut themselves, faint, get a headache, or get bitten by snakes.

I was indignant. I remember complaining to my parents that the kits were silly. Didn't anyone ever look inside these kits? My mother listened thoughtfully and then asked, "What items do you want in a kit?" I didn't know. That was the point of looking at all of those kits. I wanted to learn how to be prepared by seeing the items other people chose. She then asked, "What things happened when you were inside, outside, or playing or at school?"

That helped! Be prepared for what you have experienced or seen. I knew what I had experienced. I had splinters—so I would include a needle, matches to sterilize the needle, and tweezers to pull out the splinter. My mom sometimes had an upset stomach, so I would include a stomach remedy for her. I would include a pen-knife just in case someone couldn't breathe and needed a tracheotomy. (I had seen this on TV.) I also would include a set of directions to remind people what everything was for.

Now, with a few more years of experience, it is easier to think of what has happened and to anticipate what may happen on a trip. I am traveling all the time and

205

constantly coping with life's challenges. I no longer limit my thinking to what might happen in the woods.

It would be easy to assemble a huge kit that contains remedies for hundreds of problems, but that would not be convenient. After all, who wants to travel with the equivalent of a small pharmacy? Now I ask what challenges I might expect to encounter and what multi-purpose remedies will be helpful.

Multi-Purpose Remedies

Multi-purpose remedies assist with a variety of health challenges, enabling us to carry less and do more. Many herbs are multi-purpose remedies and do far more than what a simple advertisement would suggest. (Why don't we hear more about the multiple uses of herbs or other remedies? Well, for one thing, companies make more money selling us many remedies rather than a single remedy. Also, marketing experts know that we are more likely to purchase when the message is simple.)

Multi-purpose remedies are listed throughout this book. Here they are again, listed in alphabetical order. For more information, consult the index and read the relevant section.

Herbs

Cayenne pepper. Warming. Treats muscle pain, bruises. Relieves sore throat and bronchitis. Use aggressively at the beginning of cold or flu to avoid the illness. Stimulates the heart, treats collapse, coma. Clears digestive congestion. Stops internal and external bleeding. Do NOT use internally when pregnant, when there are bladder problems, or for non-respiratory inflammation.

Comfrey. Number one remedy to accelerate all wound healing (but read the cautions). Heals ulcers. Relieves dryness and relieves fatigue. Reduces inflammation and pain. Fabulous remedy to stop bleeding, anywhere in the body.

Echinacea root. Number 1 remedy for reducing viral and bacterial infection and fever and inflammation. Excellent epidemic preventative. External antiseptic. Treats many poisons: internal and external remedy for snake bites. Assists with boils and many skin conditions, including gangrene and septic ulcers. Stimulates digestion. Detoxifying.

Ginger. Number one remedy for treating motion sickness and nausea. Treats indigestion, food poisoning, and stomach, abdominal, and menstrual cramps. Stimulates digestion, stops vomiting. Warming. Stops diarrhea from cold. Helps pain of arthritis, sore muscles. Use aggressively at the beginning of cold or flu to avoid the illness. Relieves colds. General anti-infective and epidemic preventative.

Rhodiola. Number 1 herbal remedy to prevent and relieve altitude sickness. Energy tonic, stimulates immunity, clears lung phlegm. Cooling and drying adaptogen.

Siberian ginseng. Energy tonic, adrenal tonic, stimulates immunity, and increases aerobic capacity.

Yin Chiao herbal combination. Fabulous remedy to boost the immune system and to fight colds, flu, and many illnesses.

Yunnan Paiyao. Number 1 stop-bleeding herb. Prepared powder made from Tienchi ginseng and other herbs. Apply externally and take internally to stop bleeding.

Essential Oils

Lavender essential oil. Number 1 remedy for burns. Relaxant that relieves anxiety and depression. Calming. External remedy for pain, itching, and insect and spider bites. Apply directly to wounds to relieve pain, disinfect, reduce inflammation, accelerate healing, and reduce scarring. Eliminates lice, scabies, and other skin parasites. Apply to linen to eliminate bedbugs. Anti-viral: Steam

MAKING A TRAVEL KIT

207

inhalation (2–4 drops in 1 cup recently boiled water) for respiratory infections including colds, flu, bronchitis, and tuberculosis.

Tea tree oil. Anti-bacterial. Anti-viral. Anti-fungal. Steam inhalation (2–4 drops in 1 cup recently boiled water) to relieve colds, flu, bronchitis, and throat problems. 1 drop in 4 ounces of water used as a mouthwash, relieves toothache. Can be applied directly to the skin with or without diluting. Anti-infective for skin use.

Thyme essential oil. Number 1 remedy for all respiratory infections, including colds, flu, bronchitis, and pneumonia. Anti-bacterial. Anti-viral. Steam inhalation (2–4 drops in 1 cup recently boiled water) to relieve colds, flu, bronchitis, coughs, and throat problems. Anti-fungal. Anti-parasitic. Antidotes poison, including animal and insect bites. Major restorative: clears fatigue, weakness, and nervous exhaustion. For internal use, place 1–2 drops with olive oil in a gelatin capsule, or stir 1–2 drops into a half teaspoon of honey and a quarter cup of water. One drop in 4 ounces of water used as a mouthwash relieves toothache. **Caution: Must be diluted for internal or external use.**

Homeopathics

Aconite 30c. Number 1 remedy for ailments from exposure to cold. Outstanding remedy for shock, fear, paranoia, early stages of colds, flu and many diseases (take immediately). Immediate use can stop a cold or flu. Relaxing.

Apis 30c. Outstanding remedy for red, painful, and swollen tissues, especially following a bite.

Arnica 30c. Number 1 remedy for accidents, trauma, swelling, and exhaustion. Slows bleeding.

Arsenicum 30c. Number 1 remedy for food poisoning, especially with nausea, diarrhea and vomiting. Especially helpful for anxious people.

Belladonna 30c. Outstanding remedy for fever, sunburn, and many acute inflammations. Take immediately for colds or flu, especially if accompanied by fever or you are unusually hot or have a red face. Immediate use can stop a cold or flu.

Coca 30c. Number 1 remedy for altitude sickness.

Cocculus 30c. Number 1 homeopathic remedy for motion sickness and jet lag.

Ferrum phos 30c. Number 1 remedy for the start of a cold or flu; immediate use can stop it. Slows or stops bleeding.

Ignatia 30c. Number 1 remedy for grief or loss. Enables you to continue.

Ipecac 30c. Number 1 remedy for nausea, especially nausea that is unrelieved by vomiting. Helpful for a wide range of issues accompanied by nausea. Use it to stop bleeding if accompanied by nausea or if other remedies fail to act.

Ledum 30c. Number 1 remedy for puncture wounds, including most insect and animal bites. Anti-infective. Also helpful with ankle weakness, strains, and sprains and for leg pain that is better with cold applications. Helpful for injuries with purple skin.

Nux vomica 30c. Number 1 remedy for overindulgence in food or drink.

Rhus tox 30c. Number 1 remedy for pain and stiffness from over-exertion. Take it for ailments that are better with motion and worse with rest. (When you sit too long, you stiffen up; when you move, you get limber.) May help with poison ivy and skin issues with blisters.

Veratrum album 30c. For nausea, diarrhea, and vomiting when Arsenicum fails to help.

Other Remedies

Charcoal. Internal and external anti-poison. Treats
indigestion.

Grapefruit seed extract. (GSE) Number 1 preventative
for travelers' diarrhea. Clears yeast and mold.

Rescue Remedy. Flower essence combination. Number
1 general remedy for emotional support.

Single-Purpose Remedies

Sometimes a single-purpose remedy is so outstanding
that you will choose it in place of or in addition to a multi-
purpose remedy. For example, when traveling in areas
known for contaminated water supplies where travelers
commonly develop diarrhea, I personally would bring the
drug *Imodium.* It does one thing. It does that one thing
extremely well. It stops diarrhea. Period.

You may wish to carry certain herbs, homeopathic
preparations, or essential oils as single-purpose remedies.
All of them have multiple uses but you may choose to
focus on one. For example, if you are traveling in an area
where malaria is a problem, I recommend that you bring
homeopathic *Malaria 30c* (take 1 pellet daily) and herbal
Sweet Annie tincture (take 1 dropperful 3 times per day)
beginning 3 days prior to arrival, during your stay and
for at least 7 days following departure.

Assembling Your Travel Kit

The recommendations below are based upon creating
a travel kit of reasonable size. Use the list as a start for
developing your own kit. Many of the remedies are multi-
purpose. If you commonly experience or anticipate a particular issue, I suggest that you review the relevant section
in this book and tailor the kit to meet your needs.

Comprehensive Travel Kit

Cayenne capsules

Echinacea root tincture (1 ounce) or Yin Chiao herbal combination

Ginger root tincture (1 ounce)

Rhodiola or Siberian ginseng root tincture (1 ounce)

Lavender essential oil (10 ml)

Tea tree oil or thyme essential oil (10 ml)

Yunnan Paiyao powder (4 gram bottle)

Rescue Remedy (10 ml)

Aconite 30c

Apis 30c

Arnica 30c

Arsenicum 30c

Belladonna 30c

Cocculus 30c

Ferrum Phos 30c

Ignatia 30c

Ipecac 30c

Ledum 30c

Nux vomica 30c

Rhus toxicodendron 30c

Grapefruit seed extract

Activated charcoal capsules or capsules

Vitamin C

Triple antibiotic ointment (foil packets) or herbal salve containing goldenseal or other antibiotic herbs

Imodium

Earplugs or headphones

Sleep mask

Band-aids — assorted sizes

MAKING A TRAVEL KIT

Gauze

½ inch wide paper first aid tape

Single edged razor blade or pen knife
(You cannot bring inside the plane cabin.)

Moleskin

Needle

Tweezers

1–2 empty dropper bottles: ½ or 1 ounce

Skin sanitizer — 1 ounce size

Soap (small bar)

Tissues in waterproof bag

Small lighter or one book waterproof matches
(Carry-on luggage only. Check current TSA rules when flying.)

Small flashlight with batteries

List of all medications, herbs, homeopathic
remedies, and supplements you take

Water — small container

1 copy of *The Naturally Healthy Traveler*

Consider purchasing a homeopathic travel kit. You will pay less for a 36-remedy kit than you would pay for 10 single remedies, and in the kit the remedies stay clean and organized. I think the kits are great! You still may need to purchase individual remedies, however, for special circumstances such as altitude sickness.

Here is a mini-kit that fits in your pocket:

Mini Travel Kit

Homeopathics: Aconite 30c, Arnica 30c, Arsenicum 30c, Cocculus 30c, Ledum 30c, Nux vomica 30c (½ dram or 1/16 ounce size)

Ginger tincture (1 ounce)

Tea tree essential oil (10 ml)

Activated charcoal capsules

Rescue Remedy

Band-aids

List of all medications, herbs, homeopathics, and supplements you take

1 copy of *The Naturally Healthy Traveler*

FOREIGN PHRASES

English	German	French*
acupuncture	die Akupunktur	acuponcture
acupuncturist	der Akupunkteur	acuponcteur
ambulance	die Ambulanz	ambulance (f)
antibiotic	das Antibiotikum	antibiotique (m)
asthma	das Asthma	asthme
bandage	der Verband	bande (f) pansement (m)
bite	der Biss	piqure d'insecte (f) (insect bite)
bleeding	die Blutung	saignement (m)
breathing	atmen	respiration (f)
broken	gebrochen	cassé
Chinese	chinesisch	Chinois
chiropractor	der Chiropraktiker	chiropracteur (m)
constipation	die Verstopfung	constipation (f)
dentist	der Zahnarzt	dentiste (m)
diarrhea	der Durchfall	diarrhée (f)
drugstore	die Apotheke	pharmacie (f)
emergency	der Notfall	urgence épicerie (f)
essential oils	die Aetherische Öle	les huiles essentielles (f)
fever	das Fieber	fièvre (f)
flower essences	die Blütenessenzen	essences des fleurs (f)
food	die Nahrung	aliment (m)
grocery store	das Lebensmittelgeschaeft	supermarché (m) épicerie (f)

*The letters (m) and (f) denote gender (masculine and feminine).

Spanish	Italian	Portuguese
acupuntura	agopuntura	acupuntura
acupunturista	agopunturista	acupuntor
ambulancia	ambulanza	ambulância
antibiotico	antibiotico	antibiótico
asma	asma	asma
vendaje	fascia	atadura
picadura (insect bite)	insetto	picada
echar sangre	sanguinare	sangramento
respiracion	respirazione	respirar
fracturado (bone)	turato	cassado fraturado
Chino	Cinese	chinês or chinesa
quiropractico	chiropratico	quiroprático
estrenimiento	costipazione	constipação
dentista	dentista	dentista
diarrea	diarrea	diarréia
farmacia	farmacia	farmácia
emergencia	emergenza	emergência
aceites esencials	olii essenziali	óleos essenciais
fiebre	febbre	febre
esencias florales	essenze floreali	essências de florais
comida	alimento	alimento
supermercado	supermercado	supermercado

English	German	French
herb	die Kräuter	fines herbes (f)
herb shop	das Reformhaus or das grüne Lädchen	herboristerie (f)
herbalist	der Kräuterhändler	herboriste
homeopath	der Homöopath	homéopathe
homeopathic	homöopathisch	homéopathique
homeopathy	die Homöopathie	homéopathie
massage	die Massage	massage (m)
medical doctor	der Arzt	docteur/médecin
medicine	die Medizin	médicament (m)
nurse	die Krankenschwester	infirmière (f)
osteopath	der Osteopath	ostéopathe
pain	der Schmerz	douleur (f)
restaurant	das Restaurant	restaurant (m)
sick	krank	malade
sting	stechen	piqure (f)
tea	der Tee	thé (m)
thirst	dürstig (thirsty)	soif
toilet	die Toilette	toilettes (f)
vomiting	erbrechen	vomissement (m)
water	das Wasser	eau (f)
good	gut	bon
bad	schlecht	mauvais
yes	ja	oui
no	nein	non

Spanish	Italian	Portuguese
hierba	erbe	erva
almacen de hierbas	erboristeria	loja de ervas
herborista	erborista	herborista
homeopath	omeopata	homeopata
homeopahische	omeopatico	homeopático
homeopathie	omeopatia	homeopatia
masaje	massaggio	massagem
doctor	medico	doutor
medicina	medicina	medicina
enfermera	infermiera	enfermeira
osteopata	osteopata	osteopático
dolor	dolore	dor
restaurante	ristorante	restaurante
enfermo	ammalato	doente
picadura	puntura	picada
te	té	chá
tener sed	sete	sede
retrete	gabinetto	higiênico
vomitos	vomito	vômito
agua	acqua	água
bueno	buono	bom
malo	difettoso	mau
si	si	sim
no	no	não

217

TERMS

Essential Oils

Essential oils have been used for thousands of years and are the foundation for many perfumes and for aromatherapy. An essential oil is the distilled concentrate of a plant. Essential oils are the most highly concentrated of all herbal preparations. I think of 1 drop as being equivalent to 1 ounce of herb — essential oils are strong! One drop frequently is the dose, and that is enough. Treat all essential oils with respect; most must be diluted to prevent burning. (Lavender essential oil and tea tree oil are 2 common essential oils that you can safely use undiluted and that can be safely applied directly on the skin.) Essential oils are strongly antiviral, antibiotic, and anti-fungal, making them potent alternatives to antibiotics. They are indispensable travel remedies due to their high concentration, consistent results, and easy portability. Practitioners are called aromatherapists.

Flower Essences

A flower essence is a low concentration tea (infusion) that has been further diluted in purified water (plus alcohol as a preservative). Flowers are usually used although bark or leaf may be used for some preparations. Flower essences are used to assist people with temporary or chronic emotional imbalances. The most common flower essence is Rescue Remedy, a combination of 5 flower essences. It is perfect in all high-stress situations. Most flower essences come in tiny dropper bottles. Flower essences provide rapid and gentle results without drug interactions or side effects.

Herbs

An herb is a plant, mineral, or animal that is used for healing. (Meat, bone meal, and gelatin all derive from animals.) Western herbology relies almost entirely on plants. Herbs are available in a wide variety of forms. All forms work. I personally rely on tinctures, which are extracts from herbs in alcohol and water, in glycerin, or in vinegar. Tinctures are easy to carry, easy to add to water to make tea, work very quickly, and stay fresh. Other forms include dried bulk herbs (the dried plant or plant part) which often is used for tea, tea bags, capsules (encapsulated ground bulk herbs), herbal oils (an extract from herbs in oil), salves (a herbal oil that has been solidified, usually with beeswax), and pills (ground and cooked herb molded into pill form). Practitioners are called herbalists or herbologists — you can find them by referral or by contacting an accrediting organization such as:

- American Herbalists Guild
  www.americanherbalist.com

- National Institute of Medical Herbalists
  www.btinternet.com/~nimh/

- European Herbal Practitioners Association (an umbrella organization for several accrediting organizations)
  www.users.globalnet.co.uk/~ehpa/about.htm

Homeopathic Remedies

A homeopathic remedy is an extremely low concentration preparation of a plant, mineral, or animal that is used for healing. The extremely low concentration allows the use of what otherwise would be poisonous, such as *Rhus toxicodendron* (poison oak) to clear poison ivy rash and reduce arthritic pain. Most homeo-

219

pathic remedies come in tiny pellets that dissolve under the tongue, in liquids in dropper bottles, or in a variety of skin lotions and gels. Correctly chosen, homeopathics are some of the most effective, least expensive, and easy to carry remedies. They are widely used in the United Kingdom, India, France, and other nations to treat a variety of conditions. Practitioners are called homeopaths and may be doctors of homeopathy or lay people — you can find outstanding practitioners in either group.

You can find homeopathic remedies in natural foods stores, where supplements are sold, and in pharmacies in some parts of the world. They also can be ordered online; see the Resources section for suppliers.

RESOURCES

Books

American Herbal Products Association. *Botanical Safety Handbook, 2nd Edition* (edited by Zoe Gardner and Michael McGuffin), CRC Press, 2013.

Auerbach, Paul S., Howard J. Donner, and Eric A. Weiss. *Field Guide to Wilderness Medicine.* Philadelphia, Pennsylvania: Mosby Elsevier, 2008.

Beinfield, Harriet and Efrem Korngold. *Between Heaven and Earth: A Guide to Chinese Medicine.* New York: Ballantine Books, 1991.

Balch, Phyllis A. *Prescription for Nutritional Healing, 5th Edition.* New York: Avery, 2010.

Bensky, Dan, Steven Clavey and Erich Stoger. *Chinese Herbal Medicine: Materia Medica, 3rd Edition.* Seattle, Washington: Eastland Press, 2004.

Bergner, Paul S. *The Healing Power of Ginseng and the Tonic Herbs.* Rocklin, California: Prima Publishing, 1996.

Boericke, William and Oscar. *Materia Medica with Repertory, 9th Edition.* Santa Rosa, California: Boericke & Tafel, 1927.

Buckle, Jane. *Clinical Aromatherapy: Essential Oils in Practice, 2nd Edition.* Philadelphia, Pennsylvania: Churchill Livingstone, 2003.

Caldecott, Todd. *Food as Medicine: The Theory & Practice of Food.* United States: www.foodasmedicine.ca, 2011.

RESOURCES

Castro, Miranda. *The Complete Homeopathy Handbook.* New York: St. Martin's Press, 1991.

Colbin, Annemarie. *Food and Healing.* New York: Ballantine, 1996.

Cummings, Stephen and Dana Ullman. *Everybody's Guide to Homeopathic Medicines.* New York: Penguin Books, 2004.

Davis, William. *Wheat Belly.* New York: Rodale, 2011.

Duke, James A. *The Green Pharmacy.* New York: St. Martin's Press, 1997.

Foster, Steven and James A. Duke. *A Field Guide to Medicinal Plants and Herbs of Eastern and Central North America.* Boston: Houghlin Mifflin Company, 2000.

Graedon, Joe and Teresa Graedon. *The People's Pharmacy Guide to Home and Herbal Remedies.* New York: St. Martin's Press, 2002.

Griggs, Barbara. *Green Pharmacy: The History and Evolution of Western Herbal Medicine.* Rochester: Healing Arts Press, 1997.

Haas, Elson M. *Staying Healthy with Nutrition.* Berkeley, California: Celestial Arts, 2006.

Hahnemann, Samuel. "On the Treatment of Burns," *The Lesser Writings, Reprint Edition.* Delhi: B. Jain Publishers, 2004.

Hahnemann, Samuel. *Organon of the Medical Art, 6th Edition.* (edited and annotated by Wenda Brewster O'Reilly), Palo Alto, California: Birdcage Books, 2001.

Hershoff, Asa. *Homeopathy for Musculoskeletal Healing.* Berkeley, California: North Atlantic Books, 1996.

Hoffman, David. *Medical Herbalism: The Science and Practice of Herbal Medicine.* Rochester, Vermont: Healing Arts Press, 2003.

Holmes, Peter. *The Energetics of Western Herbs, 4th Edition, Vols. I and II.* Boulder, Colorado: Snow Lotus Press, 2007 (Vol. 1) and 2006 (Vol. 2).

Jarvis, D.C. *Folk Medicine.* New York, Fawcett Crest, 1958.

Kaminski, Patricia and Richard Katz. *Flower Essence Repertory.* Nevada City, California: Flower Essence Society, 1996.

Kaptchuk, Ted J. *The Web That Has No Weaver: Understanding Chinese Medicine, 2nd Edition.* Chicago, Illinois: Contemporary Books, 2000.

Keville, Kathi. *Aromatherapy for Dummies.* Foster City, California: IDG Books Worldwide, 1999.

Khalsa, Kurta Purkh Singh and Michael Tierra. *The Way of Ayurvedic Herbs.* Twin Lakes, Wisconsin: Lotus Press, 2008.

Kushi, Michio. *Macrobiotic Home Remedies.* Tokyo: Japan Publications, 1989.

Lieberman, Shari, *The Gluten Connection.* New York: Rodale, 2007.

Maciocia, Giovanni. *The Foundations of Chinese Medicine: A Comprehensive Text for Acupuncturists and Herbalists, 2nd Edition.* Edinburgh: Churchill Livingstone, 2006.

Mars, Brigitte. *Natural First Aid.* North Adams, Massachusetts: Storey Books, 1999.

RESOURCES

RESOURCES

Moore, Michael. *Medicinal Plants of the Desert and Canyon West.* Santa Fe, New Mexico: Museum of New Mexico Press, 1990.

Murphy, Robin. Homeopathic Clinical Repertory, 3rd Edition. Blacksburg, Virginia: Lotus Health Institute, 2006.

Murphy, Robin. *Nature's Materia Medica, 3rd Edition.* Blacksburg, Virginia: Lotus Health Institute, 2006.

Panos, Maesimund B. and Jane Heimlich. *Homeopathic Medicine at Home.* New York: Penguin Putnam, Inc., 1980.

Pitchford, Paul. *Healing with Whole Foods: Oriental Traditions and Modern Nutrition, 3rd Edition.* Berkeley, California: North Atlantic Books, 2003.

Planck, Nina. Real Food: *What to Eat and Why.* New York: Bloomsbury Publishing, 2006.

Pollan, Michael. *Food Rules: An Eater's Manual.* New York: Penguin Books, 2009.

Price, Weston A. *Nutrition & Physical Degeneration, 6th Edition.* La Mesa, California: Price-Pottenger Nutrition Foundation, 2000.

Ratey, John. *Spark: The Revolutionary New Science of Exercise and the Brain.* New York: Little, Brown & Company, 2008.

Rose, Jeanne. *The Aromatherapy Book.* Berkeley, California: North Atlantic Books, 1992.

Ross, Julia. *The Diet Cure, Revised Edition.* New York: Penguin Books, 2012.

Roy, Ravi and Carola Lage-Roy. *Homeopathic Guide for Travelers.* Berkeley, California: North Atlantic Books, 2010.

Scheffer, Mechthild. *Bach Flower Therapy: Theory and Practice*. Rochester, Vermont: Healing Arts Press, 1988.

Sisson, Mark. *The Primal Blueprint*. Malibu, California: Primal Nutrition, Inc., 2012.

Shanahan, Catherine and Luke Shanahan. *Deep Nutrition: Why Your Genes Need Traditional Food*. Lawai, Hawaii: Big Box Books, 2009.

Taubes, Gary. *Good Calories, Bad Calories: Fats, Carbs, and the Controversial Science of Diet and Health*. New York: Random House, 2008.

Tierra, Lesley. *Healing with the Herbs of Life*. New York: Crown Publishing Group, 2003.

Tierra, Michael and Lesley Tierra. *Chinese Traditional Herbal Medicine, Vols. 1 & 2*. Twin Lakes, Wisconsin: Lotus Press, 1998.

Tierra, Michael. *Planetary Herbology*. Twin Lakes, Wisconsin: Lotus Press, 1992.

Valnet, Jean. *The Practice of Aromatherapy: A Classic Compendium of Plant Medicines & Their Healing Properties* (edited by Robert Tisserand). Rochester, Vermont: Healing Arts Press, 1990.

Weil, Andrew. *Eating Well for Optimum Health*. New York: Quill, 2001.

Williams, Roger. *Nutrition Against Disease*. New York: Bantam, 1973.

Winston, David and Steven Maimes. *Adaptogens: Herbs for Strength, Stamina, and Stress Relief*. Rochester, Vermont: Healing Arts Press, 2007.

Wolf, Robb. *The Paleo Solution*. United States: Victory Belt Publishing, 2010.

RESOURCES

Worwood, Valerie Ann. *The Complete Book of Essential Oils & Aromatherapy.* Novato, California: New World Library, 1991.

Websites & Apps I Like

For helpful travel information and travel products:

www.cdc.gov/travel. Provides current health and disease information for worldwide travel.

www.gethuman.com. Website and free app that tells you the fastest way to reach a human operator on the phone. This often is faster than standing in a customer service line when your plane is canceled.

www.mdtravelhealth.com. Current and destination specific travel health information for physicians and travelers. Includes information concerning recommended medications.

www.minimus.biz. Travel-sized products.

www.rei.com. Great travel gear.

www.state.gov/travel. Travel information from the U.S. Department of State. Includes passport, embassy, and emergency information and links.

www.tsa.gov. Transportation Security Administration (TSA) website. It helps to check the current rules and procedures.

www.translate.google.com. Website and free app that translates words and phrases among more than 60 languages.

www.travmed.com. Carries a wide range of health related travel supplies, including mosquito nets, first aid and dental kits, and water treatment.

www.tripit.com. Website and app that turn flight, hotel and car emails into a printable itinerary.

www.who.int/ith/en. World Health Organization. Information on health risks and precautions for international travel.

www.wikitravel.com. Free, worldwide travel guide. This is an on-going project.

*For information about food
and food and drug sensitivities:*

www.celiactravel.com/cards. Provides restaurant cards in at least 51 languages, that you can print out and take with you when you travel, to avoid eating gluten.

www.eatwellguide.org. Provides links to local, sustainable and organic food throughout the United States.

www.epocrates.com. Free online and mobile app for drug actions, interactions, side effects and dosing.

www.gluten.net. Gluten Intolerance Group. Provides information on getting started on a gluten-free diet. Also has links to local support groups, restaurants, medical professionals and recipes.

www.glutenfreetravelsite.com. Gluten-free dining and travel reviews.

www.localharvest.org. Links to food providers, farmers, food markets and food events. I find this site invaluable for finding fresh food and local markets when I travel.

www.marksdailyapple.com. Mark's Daily Apple: Primal food, exercise and lifestyle.

www.selectwisely.com. Translation cards in multiple languages, addressing a wide range of food sensitivities and medical conditions. Get the "strongly worded" cards.

www.triumphdining.com. Gluten-free grocery and restaurant guide books, dining cards and stickers.

www.westonaprice.org. The Weston A. Price Foundation. Traditional food, farming and healing.

For information about herbs and herbal products:

www.americanherbalistsguild.com. American Herbalists Guild. Accreditation for professional herbalists. Find herbal practitioners and herbal education.

www.herbalgram.org. Home of the American Botanical Council. Herbal medicine information.

www.herbalist-alchemist.com. Herbal products and education.

www.herb-pharm.com. Huge selection of liquid herbal extracts.

www.planetherbs.com. East West School of Planetary Herbology. Blogs, articles, products (especially Chinese based formulas), discussion, current health news.

www.swsbm.com. Michael Moore's Southwest School of Botanical Medicine site. Website provides an astonishing amount of free information on herbs and herbal medicine, including books in pdf format.

For homeopathy information and products:

www.helios.co.uk. Manufacturer and seller of homeopathy kits, including a 36 remedy travel kit. Located in Kent, England.

www.homeocard.com. Possibly the world's smallest homeopathic kit – wallet sized.

www.homeopathyworld.com. Sells homeopathy kits in the U.S., including a 36 remedy travel kit.

www.nationalcenterforhomeopathy.org. National Center for Homeopathy. Find and choose a qualified homeopath, research, conferences, articles.

www.a2zhomeopathy.com. Natural Health Supply. Homeopathic remedies, kits, books and supplies.

ABOUT THE AUTHOR

Susan W. Kramer was born in Brooklyn, New York, and grew up in Perth Amboy, New Jersey, where she spent much of her time outdoors, active in sports and fascinated by the plants she discovered while tramping through the woods behind her home. After completing high school, she attended New College in Sarasota, Florida, and Marlboro College in Marlboro, Vermont, graduating from New College with a degree in economics and music. She earned an M.A. in economics and demography and a Ph.D. in economics, both from Duke University, taught economics at the College of William and Mary and George Washington University, and worked as an economist first for the Federal Reserve Board of Governors and then for the U.S. House of Representatives. She returned to the College of William and Mary to study law and practiced law for 10 years, specializing in bankruptcy litigation.

Her lifelong interests in health and plants eventually led to advanced studies, and later teaching, at East West School for Herbology in Santa Cruz, California. She became accredited as a professional member of the American Herbalists Guild (AHG) and became certified as a classical homeopath (CCH) by the Council for Homeopathic Certification. She is a registered member of the North American Society of Homeopaths (NASH) and the National Center for Homeopathy. She lives in Atlanta, Georgia, where she maintains a practice as a therapeutic herbalist, homeopath, and speaker.

A longtime competitive athlete, Kramer has earned a second degree black belt in Bu Kyoku Ryu karate and is a certified instructor of tai chi and a championship fencer. Martial arts and fencing provided her numerous opportunities for travel. Whether by bike in Sardinia, train in Mongolia, hiking in Switzerland, or cruising the oceans anywhere, Kramer is happy traveling. To celebrate her 50th birthday, she successfully climbed Mt. Kilimanjaro. She continues to train with a combination of walking, cardio, and resistance exercise, anticipating her next adventure, because, she says, "you've got to be ready!"